There are very few Americans who fully understand the workings of our legislative process. It is not that the process is so complicated; most of us just are not interested enough. There are powerful interests that are represented in Washington, and there are people who have their say to their congressmen, who often get their way simply because no other voice is heard. In the VOTER'S GUIDE TO ENVIRONMENTAL POLITICS, Garrett De Bell and the contributors spell out what needs to be done to turn things around; to make other voices heard—before, during, and after the election.

MORE BALLANTINE BOOKS YOU WILL ENJOY

SCIENCE & SURVIVAL $1.25
Barry Commoner

An eminent scientist warns against the dangers we face from new scientific technologies which have harmful long-range effects on our environment. An urgent message from the man *Time* called "the Paul Revere of ecology."

THE POPULATION BOMB 95¢
Dr. Paul Ehrlich, *A Sierra Club/Ballantine Book*

The book you can't afford not to read! Over-population is with us now and will be the root cause of major world problems unless it is brought under control. This book tells what can be done—and what is likely to occur.

THE FRAIL OCEAN 95¢
Wesley Marx, *A Sierra Club/Ballantine Book*

"A fascinating and important book. The obvious comparison is with Rachel Carson's *Silent Spring*, and I can only hope Mr. Marx's book will be as widely read, and have a comparable impact."
—*New York Times*

MOMENT IN THE SUN 95¢
Robert and Leona Train Rienow, *A Sierra Club/Ballantine Book*
"Man's destruction of his own habitat has never been so dramatically presented . . . a blockbuster of a book."
—*San Francisco Chronicle*

THE USER'S GUIDE TO THE PROTECTION OF THE ENVIRONMENT $1.25
Paul Swatek, *A Friends-of-the-Earth/Ballantine Book*

The indispensable guide to making every purchase count. Daily decisions you can make that will improve or deteriorate the environment: brand names, products, where to get those products which are ecologically safe.

THE ENVIRONMENTAL HANDBOOK: Prepared for the First National Environmental Teach-In—Edited by Garrett De Bell, *A Friends-of-the-Earth/Ballantine Book* 95¢

The 1970's is our last chance for a future that makes ecological sense. This handbook focuses on some of the major problems of our deteriorating environment, explains the nature of ecology and—most importantly—suggests action that can be taken right now in any community, by any individual.

To order by mail, send price of book plus 5¢ for postage to Dept. CS, Ballantine Books, Inc., 36 West 20th Street, New York, New York 10003. Include your order with your address and zip code.

THE VOTER'S GUIDE TO ENVIRONMENTAL POLITICS
Before, During and After the Election

Edited by Garrett De Bell

Foreword
by
David Brower

A FRIENDS OF THE EARTH/BALLANTINE BOOK
An Intext Publisher

FRIENDS OF THE EARTH, founded in 1969 by David Brower, is a non-profit membership organization streamlined for legislative activity in the United States and abroad aimed at restoring the environment misused by man and at preserving remaining wilderness where the life force continues to flow freely.

FRIENDS OF THE EARTH in order to fight without restrictions does not wish to be tax-deductible and for that reason has special need for and invites your participation.

Addresses:

FRIENDS OF THE EARTH

30 East 42nd Street
New York, N.Y. 10017

451 Pacific Avenue
San Francisco, California 94133

917 15th Street, N.W.
Washington, D.C. 20005

1372 Kapiolani Blvd.
Honolulu, Hawaii 96814

P.O. Box 1977
Anchorage, Alaska 99501

Copyright © 1970 by Garrett De Bell

SBN 345-02059-6-095

First Printing: October, 1970

Printed in the United States of America

BALLANTINE BOOKS, INC.
101 Fifth Avenue, New York, N.Y. 10003

HC
110
.E5
V65

Contents

Foreword *by David Brower*   vii

Introduction   1

Part I: THE ENVIRONMENTAL ISSUES

Chapter 1	Recycling *by Garrett De Bell*	11
Chapter 2	Transportation and America's Environment *by Robert C. Fellmeth*	22
Chapter 3	Air Pollution: Moving Beyond Motherhood *by John C. Esposito*	36
Chapter 4	Less Power to the People *by Garrett De Bell*	52
Chapter 5	Give Pesticide Policy an Ecological Conscience *by Harrison Wellford*	57
Chapter 6	A Bill of Rights for Wildlife *by Joan McIntyre*	74
Chapter 7	Wilderness *by Harvey Manning*	85
Chapter 8	Small Towns *by Clayton Denman*	98
Chapter 9	Toward a Stable Population *by Brenn Stilley*	106
Chapter 10	Eco-Pornography Revisited *by Thomas Turner*	115

150374

Part II: THE CONGRESS AND FEDERAL AGENCIES AND HOW TO GET THEM TO ACT

Chapter 11	Divesting the Regulatory-Industrial Complex *by Robert C. Fellmeth*	129
Chapter 12	Reforming Congress—First Order of Business *by Congressman Morris K. Udall and Congressman Paul N. McCloskey*	159
Chapter 13	How to Influence Your Congressman *by George Alderson*	180
Chapter 14	Become a Lobbyist for the Environment *by Garrett De Bell*	197
Chapter 15	Understanding Congressional Voting Records *by Richard Meeker*	211
	How Your Congressman Voted *League of Conservation Voters* *Friends' Committee on National Legislation*	213
Contributors		274
Appendix	What a Survival Library Can Do For You	277
	What You Can Do	281
	Conservation Coupons	305

Foreword

Introduction

The threat to the environment persists and worsens, in spite of attempts of some shallow journalists to portray concern about it as a fad, and of all too many advertising agencies to create a rug to sweep it under.

Meanwhile, back on the polluted, crowded, endangered, beautiful planet, too few antidotes to the threat have been offered us. Young people and old, new groups and traditional organizations, are working to fill the void. Garrett De Bell, one of the young people, and Friends of the Earth, one of the new groups, are here joined with Ballantine Books and the League of Conservation Voters to spell out how American voters can combine to make a difference. The American voter can learn here how to be the Ralph Nader of his block, how to effect the turnaround essential to the survival of our kind, our country, and the planet.

Before, During and After Elections: Room for Progress

Voting in elections, important as it is, is not enough. The concerned citizen must help to determine the array of candidates he selects from on election day; he must persuade other concerned people to get counted, before and on election day; and he must follow through after the votes are in. After election day, either your candidate or his opponent will be in office. He is not likely to be an evil, malevolent, stupid office holder, even if he is your man's opponent. He is capable of realizing that no one will vote, and no one will be elected, and that all life on the planet is threatened if technology is allowed to dictate to us when it should only seek to serve us.

A man who has chosen politics as a career and wishes to continue in it must seek a certain amount of consensus if he wants to stay in business. He must persuade enough of his fellows to vote with him or nothing will happen. And he is human enough to be able to do only a few things at a time without help. You may find him a willing recipient of good ideas for legislative progress for which support can be built—either through his own leadership, through the hard work of his limited staff, through the work of the good and bad lobbies, in the District of Columbia, or through your help as a citizen volunteer.

You, the citizen, may have been too busy to follow through. You may have felt you could not afford to join the organizations that can work night and day for your interests.

If we paused and looked around, all two hundred million of us, we might agree that too few of us have been willing to set aside time and money to insure a reasonable chance to live out our normal span. The thought hardly occurred to us that threats to environment were threats to us. There would always be room enough and time—later.

Now we know better. We need only step outside and breathe—and remember how much more enjoyable the process used to be—to realize that concern about the threat to the earth is by no means a fad. The threat is real and pervasive, and it is accelerating.

The good news—perhaps the only good news these days—is that this realization is now widespread enough to supply the necessary power for bringing about reforms. The Constitution foresaw the need for change and provided a route to change. It is possible, we in Friends of the Earth are convinced, to use the good parts of the System to beat the bad parts of the System.

Blueprint for Change

Seeking steps toward reform that could be orderly, just, and swift enough, we met with the editor of the best-selling *Environmental Handbook* in the pleasing environment of La Fonda del Sol, surrounded by reminders of the charm of native arts and crafts. We reviewed what we would like to do and what we *could* do in time for a 1970 "before, during, and after" elections program for voter support of the environment. What could the concerned citizen urge concerned leaders in government and industry to undertake to save the environment—without their committing political or corporate suicide?

We thought it would be a good idea to draw upon several of these leaders for assistance; to ask Members of Congress and candidates for election to make a commitment, and to report to the public on their responses.

We assumed that human beings concerned about racial equality and peace among men the world over understand that degradation of the planet and of its living resources—including people—is a single, all-encompassing crisis. We all breathe the same air; breathing is still strictly a do–it–yourself exercise. And no one will buy or sell, love or hate, or be white, yellow, red, brown, or black on a dead planet.

We assumed also that intelligent people with time to listen already knew full well that the crisis exists. So we would concentrate on proposing solutions needed now, feasible now, and fixable later if they needed fixing.

We wanted to accompany each of the national problems of top environmental importance with a proposal for reform. For each we would state the problem, include draft legislation to correct the problem or begin to, describe alternative ways to meet the need and show why we chose ours, and ask help on each chapter from a Member of Congress, or a candidate, or perhaps a loser in the election.

Having been in the business a while, we would post warnings in each chapter. We would suggest how the citizen could head off at the pass those who might attempt to vitiate the reforms, such as the people who take out four–color ads in national magazines to explain how their unrestrained pesticides can keep Bambi from a premature death at the hands of a nasty tick. Or those who stress how cars, too, must breathe clear air, and say their gasoline is the best thing there is for clean air. Or the people who send a salesman out on a nationwide speaking tour to push the idea that the U.S. will lose face unless it has an SST. We would be positive about this, and avoid the temptation to be snide.

A critically important section of the book would be a report on commitment, how each Member of Congress, or candidate for election, responded to a request for his views on the subjects, including a listing of the men who declined to answer. This would be a difficult, ambitious, essential part of the book—so much so that we should try to help phrase answers if asked to, and be willing to build support out in the hustings, for the right answers.

Then, taking a lead from the "What You Can Do" section of *Defoliation,* we would seek to improve upon what we invented there.

What are the Further Opportunities?

You can serve as judge of how much of the blueprint we have followed if you will also agree to help us with the next step. Our own feeling is that Garrett De Bell's achievement is superb, and that there is a superb opportunity for improvement by participating readers. We have found it difficult to come up with solutions. The stating of the problem, or restating of it, is much easier. Never underestimate the power of negative thinking: it is always easier to trip someone up than to stand him on his feet and aim him somewhere.

The Great Gap remains: the statement of Congressional commitment. We wanted specific promises to "bite the bullet" and "damn the torpedos" as opposed to glittering, evasive generality. But such commitment is not yet attainable in quantity.

We think we know why. The man in politics who becomes too predictable has given away in advance one of his greatest powers, his ability to trade. Call it logrolling if you are a spectator; but call it the preservation of essential flexibility if you are a participant in the legislative area and would like to keep on participating. If you are a spectator, it occurs to us, you should not accuse a man in office of being too cynical about committing himself early until you have exhausted your own imagination—and your own pen and voice—in making it possible for him to be bolder and to lean your way oftener.

Obstacles to Commitment

The routes to making greater boldness possible have many strange roadblocks. Some of the worst obstacles of all are in the Internal Revenue Code.

My own experience convinces me that one of the worst threats to the environment is the present interpretation of the tax laws. The threat is epitomized in what the Internal Revenue Service did to the Sierra Club in the club's attempt to save the Grand Canyon from two proposed power dams. Both dams would be highly destructive; neither was necessary. They would have alienated public property, and destroyed the heart of one of the earth's scenic wonders in the process. Yet the organization that led the defense of the public interest and the saving of the Grand Canyon was, in effect, fined half a million dollars for its effort. The intimidation of traditional conservation organizations gravely weakened their power just when the threat to the environment required that power more than ever before.

The conservation movement is still in that bind.

For reasons that used to be good enough, the I.R.S. encourages the creation of profit which it can tax to support the government. We are not arguing here against taxes; they are our annual deductible contribution to the cost of keeping the U.S. going.

But this approach has left conservationists in peril. Established for public purpose, they could not pursue that purpose in legislative effort—and conservation begins in legislation, is nourished by it, and dies in it—if that effort were "substantial". Webster thinks that something is 'substantial' when it has substance. It is obvious that conservation can not be of enough force if it has no substance.

Whatever the I.R.S. thinks substance means, it will not say. Conservation organizations have had to risk their own guess of what the I.R.S. means. To save the Grand Canyon, the Sierra Club took that risk, and I.R.S. took away the club's status. Other organizations could not fail to note the loss.

The need is for (1) clear wording of the law, (2) clear guidelines in the regulations, and (3) clear interpretation following adjudication, that will allow the organizations to do what they must. Those groups that have been established to speak for an otherwise voiceless environment, and that do indeed so speak in the public interest, must be allowed to pursue their purpose through any of the three branches of government, or all of them. And they must be permitted to do so without peril to the public assistance they indirectly receive through being tax-exempt and tax-deductible. They must also be able to comment openly about the environmental promises and practices of office-holders and office-seekers.

Until this clarity comes, there will be organizations like Friends of the Earth that accept the financial handicap of not being able to seek deductible funds, and do as well as they can. Forgive us for thinking it grossly unfair to have to scrape hard for tiny contributions to finance our effort to save the environment on the one hand, while on the other hand institutions and industries threatening the environment can deduct their costs of influencing the public and the legislators from *Income before Taxes*.

There are many other tax threats to the environment, such as those tax laws that discourage keeping parts of the environment open, wild, and beautiful. But the tax threat against the people who would band together to get the strength to save the land is certainly a major threat. It is second only to the threat inherent in the still-too-common assumption that more and more people can accelerate their demands upon a finite environment in search of an ever-higher standard of living without demeaning or eradicating standards for life.

Your Role in Building Support for Good Men

Early tax reform is essential and—with public support—feasible. It will allow conservation organizations to build public support for sound environmental measures. This in turn will encourage men in politics to risk an unmitigated, open commitment to the environment, and to save their trading of votes for less important concerns.

It is important to remember that the present system is devised to give men in political life the maximum opportunity of re-election. This is an opportunity of which they think highly. Those of us who do not want to enter that life and assume the chores of holding office are nevertheless entitled to protest vigorously the inequities of the present system. We can do so most effectively if we have also worked creatively to build public support for the political leaders who support governmental reform on behalf of the environment.

Citizens working on behalf of the environment need the strength that comes from alliance. They need the good conservation conservative. They need the newcomer to environmental concern, who must be found in all colors and fields. They need the responsible corporation executive who, although he has not always worked wisely, has often worked hard, and has the ability to lead on better routes when he discerns them. We need to coalesce, not to splinter, in behalf of the environment.

In attempting to initiate a new growth of citizen activity we have inevitably set forth as new ideas concepts that are merely new to us, but old and tried before by those who have toiled long in the vineyard to rescue and defend the beautiful places we have inherited. If some of what is said here sounds too enthusiastic, please remember that it is better to be naive than to be null. Remember too that at the present disastrous rate of population growth there are enough people added to the world every three years to populate a new United States, and none of them has yet heard what you have heard. Let good things be heard more.

Your Role as an Editor

What could a book like this do better? Where has it succeeded best? The margins are wide, and there are intentional blanks and coupons. Forgetting for a moment that *survival* is an overworked word and remembering that it is an underworked practice, let this be your (political) survival workbook. Mark it up. In the margins, correct the ideas you don't like. Underline and quote those you do. Add yourself; your own genius, the power of your life. If you have time, let us know what we can say better next time. We may agree. We will listen.

Several pages show how you may amplify your voice by adding your force to that of others whose ideas are close to yours. Join with others for strength. If you belong only to your own–personal–self club, you limit yourself too much.

Value, if you will, the diversity—the essential diversity—of the organizations that try to stand guard for you when other duties consume your time. Support several of them. A dozen may not be too many; the cost of a beer or of a pack of cigarettes a day would support that many organizations and would make survival part of your budget.

The Survival Office in Your House

We have some suggestions for your consideration:

Build a survival library and a Write–your–Congressman–and–Editors room in some nook of your house.

Write in this book and tear appropriate pages out of it. At very little cost we can supply another.

Gather a few friends in your house to help do these things if you'd rather not be alone in the effort. Your house could be the local office of Friends of the Earth. Ask about it!

Make the next version of this book better if you have time to.

Make the next election a better one for your having followed up on the current one, with whatever ideas this book has given you or which you have given us.

We do not underestimate your power, and hope *you* don't.

The first goal, let us suggest, is to predict a tenable future for this planet, and then to marvel at what a big difference your own concerted effort will make. Remember Rachel Carson—who did her homework, minded her English, and *cared*.

There are many variants of a few irrefutable themes to develop in the course of persuading good people to change course:

1) *Man has not yet had time to learn enough.* In the week of Creation (using *Genesis* time), man arrived only three minutes before midnight on the sixth day, upon a world that had worked quite well without him all the previous week.

2) *Progress does not consist of ever-increasing speed,* whether it be of air travel, of the using up of coal, oil, and gas, of the pollution of air, or of the broadcasting of poisonous chemicals that the environment has not learned to cope with.

3) *There are limits.* We cannot constantly double anything. We can let technology grind its way through the last bit of natural beauty and wildness and then be forced to turn around and repair our damage. Or we can, as rational beings, turn around sooner while there is still natural beauty and wildness around us serving purposes we may some day be wise enough to understand.

4) *In diversity is strength.* Biological stability, beauty, and wealth derive from complexity.

For example, if somehow the Appalachian forests had been simplified to chestnut, the blight would have obliterated the forest. But there was diversity, not a monoculture; although the chestnut is gone, we still have the forest. The lesson is almost unheeded. We can learn it now.

5) *Man often forgets his second great attribute.* Through the ages he has aggressively manifested his territoriality. He has also manifested love, the inexhaustible resource.

Conclusion

Any of the foregoing that sounds didactic was written either out of habit or out of guilt, but that does not purge it of validity. Thoreau said "What is the use of a house if you haven't got a tolerable planet to put it on!" The push for a tolerable planet is on!

David R. Brower

Berkeley, California
August 18, 1970

Send responses or suggestions to:
David Brower or Garrett De Bell
c/o Friends of the Earth
451 Pacific Avenue
San Francisco, Calif. 94133

ACKNOWLEDGMENTS

Many people were indispensable in making the preparation of this book fun as well as feasible:

Richard Meeker, who helped assemble the voting records and information on groups, and gave valuable help in editing and proofing.

Elayne Janiak, who did the tedious job of typing the manuscript and whose Freudian typos were always entertaining.

Bud, whose sparkling company made the long hours in the preparation of this book more mellow.

Brenn Stilley, who did extensive rewriting and editing on many of the pieces. He takes full irresponsibility for the outrageous puns in this book.

David Brower, whose vision and poetry inspired the movement when eco—catastrophe was but a gleam in the technologist's eye. He helped shape the idea of this book and arranged for its publication.

Keith Murray, who has been a continuing source of good ideas and helpful criticism.

the many Congressional aides, whose information and critical discussions were invaluable.

my wife, Suzy, who provided aid and comfort to friend and FOE, and critically reviewed all our ideas. Sometimes, in fact, very critically.

GARRETT DE BELL

Introduction

by Garrett De Bell

In *The Environmental Handbook,* we tried to provide an overview of the environmental crisis and a sampling of views on how to avert disaster and develop an ecologically sound society.

This book is an expanded look at one approach—*federal legislation.* Wherever possible, we have proposed specific legislation for specific problems, from wilderness preservation to the recycling of garbage. But proposed legislation and general goals are only a part of what must be done. There have been good ideas in the wind for years which have never been planted in successful bills and germinated into social change.

Much of this book therefore is devoted to reforms which are needed in our institutions, particularly the United States Congress and regulatory agencies.

It is vital to grasp the connection between the quality of our lives and the internal rules of Congress and congressionally established agencies, which often stifle needed reform. Numerous exposés of the "environmental crisis" have convinced people that cars produce smog and that the SST will make a hell of a racket. But there is rarely any mention of institutional causes such as the seniority system, the secrecy of committee votes in the House of Representatives, the lack of enforcement provisions in the Freedom of Information Act, and the stifling of regulatory agencies by the implied bribe of future employment in the "regulated" industry.

Much of *The Environmental Handbook* concerned new life styles more compatible with the world's eco-system than present patterns of manipulated and conspicuous consumption, so evident in all our gadgets and labor-saving appliances. In this new life style, walking and bicycling would replace cars for short hops, trains would be used for longer trips, with leisurely boat voyages substituted for today's hectic jet flights to Europe. This sort of change is desirable, and certainly more basic than legislating reform.

But unless Congress and state and local governments begin to embody sound environmental principles in the laws and regulations which govern our society, about the only way anyone will be able to live ecologically will be to "drop out" so far that they thereby lose all possibility of promoting change in the parent American culture. There is some evidence that this is already happening, with many "eco-freaks" moving to communes in wilderness or rural areas. Their efforts are all to the good;

but meanwhile, the United States as a whole continues to ruin the continent, and contribute to wrecking much of the rest of the world.

It is often said that environmental problems are incredibly complicated. This usually comes as a prelude to recommendations for more research, or establishment of a study commission to investigate the problem and issue a report. Well, the problems *are* complicated—if you try to solve them without making any fundamental changes. Ending air pollution without stabilizing power use, phasing out the internal combustion engine, and developing mass transit systems is unlikely, if not impossible. Feeding the world's population without stopping population growth is equally doubtful. All the technological schemes for increasing food supply result in more damage to the environment. The pesticides used to boost food production kill the larvae of fish and crabs and make many types of fish too poisonous to eat.

The Aswan Dam is supposed to boost food production by irrigating the desert, but it deprives the lower lands of their annual layer of fertilizing silt, while reducing fish catches in the Mediterranean by trapping nutrients behind the dam. This repetitive story is the trademark of narrow technologists who see all the benefits of their schemes, but always ignore the side effects downstream, downwind, or next year.

Some of this book's chapters deal with specific legislative proposals, while others are more general. This is because the "state of the art" varies from field to field. The question is, why are there so few constructive proposals in fields that have hundreds of "expert" practitioners in universities across the country? What are the professors of city planning and economics, for instance, doing besides grading papers? Pretty pictures of "Model Cities," and other dreamy projects are nice, but where are the realistic proposals that take the political, economic, and ecological worlds into account?

Where are the economists asking the right questions, such as how to get a workable steady-state economy, instead of one where ecologically destructive boondoggles are approved only because they provide more jobs? Which of them has been working out mechanisms for an adequate guaranteed annual income, which would break the job-income nexus which traps so many in poverty? Job training programs are inadequate, since the number of people who seek jobs is greater than the number of jobs available. Possibly the reconstitution of many universities after the Cambodian invasion will encourage graduate students to stand up to mossbacked faculty members and direct their research toward relevant questions.

The ecology movement often finds itself estranged from its bedfellows. We have continually been surprised by the negative reaction of anti-war and minority leaders, who felt that ecology represented a diversion of effort from their cause. If their anger had been directed against shucking and jiving politicians, we would have understood. Many politicians who want to end the war (with a "just" peace), and who backed the (rhetorical) War on Poverty, have now announced their firm opposition to dirty air and water. But usually anti–war and minority leaders have made no distinction between people advocating far–reaching changes and those making public relations points. The irony and tragedy of this is that the goals of minority groups, anti–war groups, and the environmental movement are compatible and often the same.

Birdwatchers have made common cause with the United Farm Workers, who recently signed contracts with grapegrowers to ban pesticides harmful to workers and wildlife. Politicians who are really good on environmental issues are, almost to a man, against the war and in tune with the aspirations of blacks, Chicanos, and American Indians.

The Senator Murphy (R-California) who supports Nixon's war policy and the SST is the same Murphy who works to end federal support to legal aid programs. On the other hand, Senator Nelson (D–Wisconsin), one of the first to call for a ban on DDT, was also an early opponent of the war. Senator McCarthy (D–Minnesota), whose anti–war credentials are well known, originated S. 3780, the only meaningful Guaranteed Annual Income proposal ("$5500 or fight"), and is working closely with the National Welfare Rights Organization for its passage.

Like *The Environmental Handbook,* this is not an "informational" book. The proposals contained herein will not just happen because they are good ideas. We have attempted to provide facts on which to base, among other things, specific questions to ask candidates for public office. General questions are often useless. We do not know of a single politician on record favoring air pollution, but there are many who oppose any measure to re-allocate the highway trust fund from highway construction to supporting a balanced transportation system. Only when the American voters can distinguish self-serving rhetoric from real commitment to reform will environmental quality improve.

Voting records on key votes are included at the back of the book, to give you an idea of how incumbent candidates have been voting. One should compare their speeches with their records.

Many people are bewildered by all the problems, all the facts, all the information to digest. The most productive approach, we feel, is to try to really grasp one area—including its biological basis, economic and political considerations, proposals in the field, your representative's position statements on the issue, his record on actual votes, and the powerful interest groups lined up on the other side. This is likely to be much more effective than a diffuse discontent about "the ecological crisis."

We have heard a good deal of cynicism around about solving problems "within the system." There is good reason for it. It is difficult to understand the intransigence of a system which has been unable to end the Indochina war, poverty, racial discrimination, urban deterioration, air and water pollution; a society which doesn't have the money to provide enough hospitals or sewage treatment plants, but has plenty to spare for ABMs, moon shots, and supersonic transports. It would appear that the politicians aren't really *opposed* to survival. It's just that it isn't politically feasible this year.

Yet this book is based on the idea that survival *is* politically feasible—and if it isn't, we'd damned well better make sure that it becomes so. The possibilities are there. Many of the key votes in the Congress carry by tiny margins, so the election of a few more supporters could mean the difference.

The SST passed the House by a bare 14 votes (out of 435 representatives) this year. Last year's margin was 62 votes. What caused the change were the efforts of the few environmental lobbyists in Washington supported by the letter writing, phone calls, editorials by citizens and groups across the country.

Many Senators and Representatives were themselves elected by very small margins. Arizona's reactionary Senator Fannin, and Murphy of California were last elected by less than a two per cent margin. A small effort could have turned the tide. Some races are even closer: Senator Cannon of Nevada won by 48 votes.

This November's elections offer an opportunity to keep the good incumbents in office; with most money and support needed for those such as Senator Hart of Michigan, and Tydings of Maryland, who face strong or organized opposition. But there are also areas where good, strong candidates are challenging do-nothing incumbents (e.g., Phillip Hoff's attempt to unseat Senator Prouty of Vermont), with a chance of picking up seats. Readers who want to campaign for candidates should consult the listing of groups in the back for information on organizations which can put them in touch with good candidates who need help in registering voters, precinct work, and so forth.

It will take a sustained effort, particularly in the 1970 and 1972 elections, to replace the do-nothings with environmentally sound legislators.

The idea is not new. It is called Democracy, and sometimes it works.

PART I

THE ENVIRONMENTAL ISSUES

Chapter 1

Recycling

by Garrett De Bell

Garbage is now in the public eye. Photographic essays of smoldering dumps, auto graveyards, and littered beaches, parks, and roadsides have reached every household in America. Everyone is aware that solid waste ranks with air and water pollution as a severe public problem, and that its disposal contributes to these problems.

The amounts of solid waste produced in the United States are staggering. A 1960 report on "Solid Waste Management" prepared for the Office of Science and Technology of the Executive Office of the President shows that the per capita production of waste each day in the United States includes seven pounds of urban solid waste and garbage, three pounds of industrial waste, and 58 pounds of agricultural waste consisting of 15 pounds of vegetable and 43 pounds of animal wastes. A look at a single family's weekly accumulation of garbage should be enough to convince anyone that the solid waste problem is severe. All this stuff has to go somewhere.

Unfortunately, industry has regarded solid waste disposal primarily as an image problem to be solved by their public relations departments. The environmental teach–ins across the country in April, 1970, often focused on litter, particularly no-deposit, no-return bottles and cans—a small, but conspicuous, part of the solid waste problem. Soft drink and beer bottlers and canners, criticized for producing non–refillable containers, responded in two ways. First, they established a public relations campaign designed to show their new–found ecological conscience: Please–don't–litter slogans were printed on beer cans and hip musical television commercials proclaimed, "The problem isn't our bottles, it's the litterbugs who give our product a bad name." Litterbugs *are* a problem, but the real problem is that we have a system producing vast quantities of consumer goods with no adequate system to deal with them after they become waste.

The second industry response has been reform–oriented, though of limited scope. Reynolds Aluminum and, more recently, the Glass Container Manufacturers Institute have announced the establishment of reclamation centers where aluminum cans and glass bottles may be redeemed for one–half cent each. Their effect is commendable, at least as a test of the economic and technical problems of recycling the aluminum and glass. Unfortunately, the amounts of aluminum and glass reclaimed by these efforts are so far very small and will probably remain so. The main benefit of such projects is, once again, a good image for the companies.

Most ecologists recognize that the solution to the solid waste problem lies in producing less waste and in recycling what is produced. Recycling involves processing and then returning wastes either to industry as raw materials (iron, steel, paper, aluminum, glass) or to the land where they came from (composted organic garbage, feed-lot manure, food-processing or field waste). The knowledge necessary to recycle much of our solid waste is already available.

Aluminum is a good example. This valuable metal is easy to recycle because it needs only to be resmelted. Aluminum scrap in the form of all-aluminum cans is worth $200 a ton—ten times the value of scrap iron or paper. The benefits of recycling aluminum are:

> Each ton of aluminum cans recycled is a ton of cans that doesn't have to be dumped into a landfill or end up on the roadside.

> Each ton of aluminum produced from scrap means that four tons of bauxite (raw ore) don't have to be imported or mined and processed in this country or mined and shipped from elsewhere (86% of our bauxite is imported, mainly from Jamaica). This would eliminate about 50 dollars of overseas expenditures for each ton produced from recycled cans.

> Each ton of aluminum produced from recycled aluminum saves about 16,000 KWH of electric

power used in the electrolytic process that converts bauxite to aluminum, and avoids the resulting pollution.

Each ton of aluminum produced from recycled aluminum means that three tons of byproduct mineral wastes don't have to be disposed of in our rivers or elsewhere.

Obviously, the potential advantages to society from recycling aluminum alone, are great. *Why, then, isn't aluminum generally collected and recycled?*

The answer is that private industry has little economic incentive at present to recycle any but the most valuable and concentrated wastes.

Look again at the list of advantages recycling aluminum would bring about. Notice that most of the costs which recycling eliminates are *social* costs, which are not borne by the manufacturer. Society as a whole, not the company, pays for garbage dumps, for picking up cans from the roadside, for pollution from the production of the power that goes into making more cans. It costs the company next to nothing to dump its byproducts into the environment.

On the other hand, the manufacturer *would* have to pay at least something for having the used cans collected, cleaned, sorted, and delivered to the smelter. The result is that, except for "window dressing," it has not generally been considered worth an industry's while to recycle.

The same situation applies to all waste materials. Organic garbage and stockyard manures, when properly treated (often by composting) and returned to the soil, improve soil quality and reduce the need for chemically produced fertilizers. Because they retain nutrients better than the powerful inorganic fertilizers, they do not contribute to the deterioration of ground water quality by increasing nitrate levels, as do the powerful chemical fertilizers. At present, a farmer in need of fertilizer simply compares the cost of recycled manure and the chemical additives often needed to supplement it, with the lesser cost of chemical fertilizer. Since the all–chemical type is cheaper, he uses it. But the farmer doesn't pay for the deterioration he causes in the ground water which, in many areas, is now undrinkable.

The social cost of pollution caused by disposing of the manure, sewage sludge, and garbage also does not enter into a city's policy of not recycling. Off New York City there are 20 square miles of ocean bottom so full of sewage sludge, and garbage that shell fish for miles around are contaminated and unfit for human consumption.

In other words, for the farmer to maximize profit and the city to minimize costs, we use a system that, overall, is much more costly to society and destructive of environmental quality than is composting the garbage, sludge and manures and returning them to the soil. With adequate legislation, our garbage bills might go up by the amount needed to subsidize the sale of the resultant fertilizer to make it competitive with chemical fertilizer. At the same time, though, we wouldn't have pollution of groundwater resources and the ocean or the estuarine and continental shelf waters either.

LEGISLATIVE PROPOSALS TO ENCOURAGE RECYCLING OF WASTES

Clearly then, recycling represents the most ecologically sound alternative to current practices of dumping, burning, or burying wastes, which add to the burden of pollution, and waste resources. What kind of legislation could give recycling a boost?

To begin with, it must be based on the premise that no one has a "right" to pollute, or to impose the costs of pollution on the public. Any harm to the general welfare arising from the production, use, or disposal of goods must be paid by those responsible for it—the manufacturers and users of a product—not those who suffer from it. Payment could be extracted in the form of a tax or fee.

The most common legislative proposals in this area fall into two general categories. They might be described as pollution taxes and disposal taxes.

Pollution or effluent taxes would require companies to compensate the public for polluting air and water which belong to everyone. For companies which dump their waste products into a nearby stream, this would mean a series of charges levied against them for use of the stream, on a per–pound basis. The more they dump, the more they would pay.

The real intention of this plan is not to make the companies provide financial compensation —since the environment they are damaging is beyond price—but to make it to their financial advantage to stop polluting. It should be kept in mind that most pollutants are also *resources,* which now are not quite worth the trouble to recover; the effluent tax would spur industries into finding better ways of recovering and re-using their waste products.

What revenues did come in from the pollution tax, however, could be used to subsidize forms of recycling not otherwise economically feasible or for research and development of recycling techniques.

At the time of this writing, the concepts outlined above are embodied in Wisconsin Senator William Proxmire's Regional Water Quality Act (S. 3181). The bill would establish a system of national effluent charges and develop regional agencies for planning and managing water quality on an area–wide basis.

Advantages of the proposal, according to Senator Proxmire:

"First, and perhaps most important, the imposition of such a system will enable us to make rapid strides in a relatively short time toward significantly improving the quality of our nation's waterways.

"Second, the bill places responsibility on the polluter, and not the public, for paying for damage to the environment.

"Third, the bill works toward an ultimate solution to the pollution problem by encouraging waste reduction rather than waste conversion. Since the charges would be levied on a per–pound basis, there would be a direct incentive for polluters to reduce their waste production in order that a major part of the charge would be eliminated.

"Fourth, the bill will provide substantial new sources of revenue for the construction of waste treatment facilities.

"Fifth, the bill provides strong economic incentives for the creation of regional water management associations."

Disposal taxes, the other general heading under which legislation to promote recycling falls, would charge the producer of a manufactured item an amount sufficient to make it economically feasible to collect and process the waste resulting from his product. This would particularly apply to unnecessary or unrecyclable packaging. The tax would also cover the cost of returning the recycled wastes to a raw materials pool or to the land as a soil conditioner.

Here again, the primary aim would be not so much to bring in compensatory revenue as to make it profitable for manufacturers to build products that are capable of being recycled.

Several bills before Congress in 1970 employ this disposal tax principle. Senator Gaylord Nelson, of Wisconsin, has introduced the Packaging Pollution Control Act (S. 3665). The purpose of this act is "To amend the Solid

Waste Disposal Act in order to establish economic incentives for the return, reuse, and recycling of packaging, to reduce the public costs of packaging and other solid waste disposal, to require national standards for controlling the amount and environmental quality of packaging, and for other purposes." Citizens should act to enlist support for Senator Nelson's amendment. At the same time more inclusive legislation should be proposed to deal with a greater variety of products than packaging.

There should be more research on technical problems of recycling. This year the House Interior Committee was requested to appropriate an additional $200,000 a year to speed up research on salvaging wood fibers from urban garbage for reuse at the Madison, Wisconsin, Forest Products Laboratory of the Forest Service. The Society of American Foresters and conservation groups like ZPG (Zero Population Growth) and FOE (Friends of the Earth) sponsored this request out of the shared belief that such applied research would return high dividends. The Interior Committee turned down the request. Citizens must increase pressure on Congressmen to appropriate funds for such socially valuable research, and to eliminate expenditures for such projects as the SST, the C5A, and the Indochina War.

Another proposal is needed to deal with the growing problem of abandoned automobiles and unsightly junk yards. There should be a fee or deposit of $25 on all new cars to be returned to the final owner of the car when he delivers it to a certified recycling facility. The deposit would be sufficient incentive to get most rusting cars off the streets and junk yards, into the hands of recyclers. A bill to implement this has been introduced by Senator Jacob Javits of New York (S. 3522, and in a revised form as Amendment 705 to S. 2005, the Solid Waste Disposal Act). There are technical problems of implementation still to be worked out, but the final bill (probably in the next Congress) will probably call for the fee to be paid on purchase; the registration certificate to serve as a receipt, with the deposit paid to the final owner, whether an individual, a junk yard, or a city agency, when the car is delivered to a recycler.

One general bill, S. 2005, the Resource Recovery Act introduced by Senator Muskie, in the form reported out of the Senate Public Works Committee, is a sound bill that would shift the emphasis of federal programs from the old style approaches of land fill and incineration to the ecologically sound recycling principle. It includes money for research, demonstration grants, training of personnel, and construction of facilities, as well as for research on the disposal tax and other innovative approaches.

It will be necessary to pressure the House to amend its bill to conform to the Senate bill —otherwise this act could be as useless as the previous Solid Waste Disposal Act of 1965. Unfortunately, grants under the 1965 Act have largely been spent on unproductive projects for improvements on the ecologically foolish land–fill and incinerator approaches to solid waste management. More desirable recycling projects have been lacking. A summary of such grants given out over the period June 1, 1966 through December 31, 1967, shows that only 5 of the 53 Federal grants went to projects dealing with composting, returning sewage sludge to agricultural soil, and other approaches geared to recycling. The remaining 48 grants paid for landfill and incinerator projects. It will take a steady pull to get the entrenched bureaucrats out of the dumps.

Our pollution problems can be solved if we pressure our congressmen to pass legislation designed to get at the roots of problems such as solid waste disposal, rather than skirt around them with high-sounding prose. Industry will certainly lobby against most of the proposals suggested in this chapter. We must make it clear to our representatives that to stay in office they must pass meaningful legislation.

Chapter 2

Transportation and America's Environment*

by Robert C. Fellmeth

A society's transportation system is a major determinant of its environment.

Americans have long prided themselves on their efficiency and technological know-how. Yet an examination of the transportation system in the United States today reveals that it is run by competition–choking monopolies, charges excessive and discriminatory rates, wastes resources, is the single most powerful lobbying force in the country, and maximizes population concentration and pollution. The resulting environmental deterioration boggles the imagination.

To see how this comes about, we must briefly examine how the present system works.

*For documentation of the conclusions in this article, see the author's *The Interstate Commerce Omission,* Grossman Publishers, 1970.

STRUCTURE

The competitive structure of the various modes transporting freight must be understood. The modes include railroads, motor carriers (trucking), water carriers (barges, etc.), and pipelines.

There exists little or no true competition, except *between* modes. *Within* modes, concentration or monopoly is the rule.

Mergers are common, and the Interstate Commerce Commission (ICC) approves them almost routinely. Thirty of the past 34 requests for rail mergers, and almost all motor carrier requests, have been granted. The agency has no criteria, guidelines, or policy to preserve competition. Its approval of mergers flies in the face of repeated failures to achieve promised cost savings.

The result is increasing concentration within each mode. Three rail carriers in the South carry 75% of the freight transported by rail in the region. Four carry 72% of it in the East. (These seven carriers are planning further mergers among themselves.) The number of regulated trucking concerns has shrunk from over 26,000 in 1940 to 15,125 in 1968, while volume and business have increased. Among water carriers, one carrier collects 66% of the revenue in the Great Lakes area, four carriers collect 50% on the Mississippi River, and two collect 50% in both the Pacific and Atlantic regions. Among pipelines, the top 19% of the firms control 70% of the nation's pipeline mileage.

Contrary to its legal mandate, the ICC regularly approves interlocking directorships. It discourages entry of new firms into a field where the existing companies are grossly inefficient or charge stratospheric rates. A new entrant applying for a market with the ICC will be spurned by the agency if there is a presently authorized carrier which is *potentially* able, and willing, to carry the traffic. Evidence of an applicant's superior efficiency, cost advantage, or lower rate intentions are not even *allowed* in evidence. Shippers requesting or backing a new entrant are ignored; applicants have had petitions of support from over 100 shippers, including major ones, but to no avail. Not surprisingly, large shippers often use their own private transportation, an alternative too expensive for smaller businesses.

Another way the ICC discourages competition is by its narrow definitions of commodities in authorizing routes. Even if a new competitor gets ICC approval to carry a given commodity from point X to point Y—an approval which may be limited to a given road, with business stops in transit prohibited—it may be allowed to carry *plastic* hose, but not all *flexible* hose, *unexposed* photographic paper, but not *exposed* photographic film, and so on. As a result, trucks go half-empty or bypass waiting loads, railroad box cars move for an average of two and a half hours a day.

HIGH RATES

The result of this non–competitive structure is a transportation system engaged in a perpetual orgy of monopoly power pricing.

It has already been mentioned that the ICC does compel some competition between modes. Thus, rail–truck mergers are prohibited. But within the modes, carriers are allowed to get together in various regions and collusively set prices in "rate bureaus." The ICC refuses to regulate rate bureaus, despite the explicit obligation to do so.

Any independent challenge or protest of a high price set by a rate bureau is extremely expensive and time-consuming. The ICC puts the burden of proof on the party proposing a change, even if it is protesting because the rate is unfairly high.

Rate bureaus generally set rates at a high enough level to keep solvent the most inefficient carrier in the bureau, which hardly encourages efforts to increase efficiency.

Although direct merger between competing modes is prohibited, "price leadership" is not unknown. Railroad executives have admitted that the major impediment to across–the–board increases is truck rates, and trucking executives admit the counterpart. Since 1967 there have been five major rail rate increases, most followed by a flurry of trucking rate increases. Both sets of increases far exceeded what would have been necessary to compensate for inflation.

The ICC does not examine rate increase requests carefully. In practice, the burden of proof seems to shift to those *protesting* the increase. A mere recital of rising wage costs is usually enough, and no accounting requirements are enforced, even though past cost–increase estimates have been shown to have been inflated by a factor of, in one case, six to one! *Actual* costs are not investigated.

Quite apart from ICC failure to require a minimum level of efficiency from a protected carrier with monopoly power before granting a rate increase (which would be unthinkable to the agency), it fails to recognize that rate increases are not justified purely because some costs rise. If *output* (ton–miles) increases at a comparable pace, because of advances in technology, fuels, computers, and so on, then an increase is not justified.

RATE VARIATION AND RESOURCE WASTE

Carriers vary their rates by what is known as "value–of–service" discrimination, which consists in charging rates which result in different profit levels for different types of commodities. Transportation costs are generally more significant in relation to raw materials than in relation to finished products. A five–ton carload of wheat might be worth $300, while a five-ton carload of radios would be worth $15,000. Increasing the transportation charge by one cent per ton-mile, for instance, would be trivial in the case of the radios, but might represent a huge percentage increase in the cost of raw materials.

Carriers therefore price manufactured items for very high profits, and raw materials for low or no profits. Given that, the manufacturer naturally tends to locate his plant near markets —large cities—to minimize his transportation costs.

From an environmental standpoint, the opposite would be better. It is easy to see the absurdity of wasting transportation systems and fuel in order to haul coal hundreds of miles to burn it to create steam to turn turbines to produce electricity which then travels by a clean, efficient underground cable only a few miles. Worse still, it means that plants are concentrated in or near cities, adding to urban air pollution and to population density of cities. If manufacturing plants were located near the sources of raw materials, wastes from production could be much more easily disposed of (even by such non-ecological methods as burial) than in crowded cities. Through the ICC, we are not only failing to assess manufacturers for the social costs of pollution; we are in effect subsidizing it.

In addition to this form of differential pricing, carriers also discriminate against each other. Since the only competition which exists is between different modes (water, trucking, rail, etc.), each mode jacks up its rates collusively where it has an advantage over its competing modes. It then uses these bloated profits to subsidize below-cost rates where it is at a disadvantage *vis-a-vis* the others. So for the same commodity, the profits will be much different in different geographical areas, depending upon the degree of intermodal competition.

This works in two ways. First, each mode can collusively exercise monopoly power where it has an inherent advantage for a certain commodity in given loads over a given distance. As the distance a shipment must travel increases over 200 miles, railroads have an increasing cost advantage over trucking. Look at the following table of profits for an illustrative commodity, taken from the Ralph Nader 1970 task force report on the ICC:

Direction	Clay and Bentonite Miles	Profit (Revenue/cost)
S to S	128	125
E to E	149	130
W to W	632	145
E to S & S to E	907	172
S to W & W to S	1,275	158
E to W & W to E	1,929	123

Rates are set for low profits at the short distances where trucking is somewhat competitive, and for high profits where railroads have a cost advantage. At distances beyond 1,000 miles, where competition from water carriers (barges) begins to become a factor, profits decline again.

The second basis for mode monopoly power is where there is an actual non–existence of another mode between points where traffic must be carried. There may be no rail spur line, no navigable waterway, or no interstate highway. The pattern we have already seen applies;

since there is no alternative, rates are set for exorbitant profits. Although transported under similar circumstances and comparable distances, newsprint costs 2.08 cents per mile to move where there is no water transport and 1.31 cents per mile where there is (Tennessee to Houston, Texas); coal costs 0.84 cents per ton–mile where there is no water transport and 0.50 cents per ton–mile where there is (western Kentucky to Tampa, Florida); and hydrofluoric acid costs 2.48 cents per ton–mile where there is no water transport and 1.16 cents per ton–mile where there is (Houston, Texas to Chicago).

In the latter cases, there are more plants located near water than efficiency or a competitive market (much less pollution considerations) would dictate. And in general, there is a serious misallocation of traffic among the modes. Each mode uses its monopoly power where it has an advantage to subsidize rates for traffic it is not optimally suited to carry. The most efficient mode is often driven out of the market. The resulting waste is beyond description, but some idea may be gathered from the fact that 90% of intercity trucking, according to expert estimates, is conducted under circumstances where rail is the actual low-cost mode.

PITY THE POOR PASSENGER

In contrast to freight transportation, there are almost always different modes competing for passenger traffic. Trains have several advantages over other forms of transportation—they are safer, less nerve-wracking, and (at least potentially) pleasanter for the passenger than, say, automobiles. The comfort and efficiency of European and Japanese trains is well known. Why, then, are American railroads constantly trying to get rid of their passenger service, if it might well be made profitable?

The answer is that, while passenger traffic is not unprofitable *per se,* freight transportation is *more* profitable, because of the monopolies and near-monopolies railroads often have. Where would you put your money—into operations where a reasonable profit is possible, but only with work and effort, or into operations where there is the security of assured revenues for years to come?

So railroads consciously try to downgrade passenger service; then use declining patronage to justify discontinuance of these operations. Downgrading often takes spectacular forms. One railroad hired a team to find ways to harass passengers—stopping trains en route in the middle of nowhere because a discontinuance had been awarded 10 minutes earlier, deliberately shutting off air conditioners in 95 degree heat. Cars average over 30 years in age, with little replacement. Reservations are rarely taken. Railroad advertising for passengers is 1/20 that of airlines. No effort is made to establish incentive arrangements with travel services, as airlines do. Executives in charge of passenger operations are given subordinate titles and positions.

As if that weren't enough, the competitive position of railroads is also undermined by rivalry between regulatory agencies. The Civil Aeronautics Board regulates airlines so that short–haul airlines are subsidized by the government, and long–route carriers can set rates for greater profits to subsidize short hops. Since the rail market is substantially in the under–500–mile range, this means that the airlines are allowed to use monopoly profits; or are subsidized, to undercut railroads where the latter are competitive. Government agencies act as irresponsible promoters of their constituent industries, rather than regulators.

Railroads also get short shrift in government subsidies. Aside from the initial land grants, the railroads have received little subsidization, and must pay property taxes on their privately owned rights–of–way. The more environmentally costly and dangerous trucking industry is not so hampered. Thanks to oil and automobile manufacturers' support for expenditures, the federal government will have spent 62 billion dollars by 1975, 58% of which goes to interstate highways. State and local governments, attracted by 30–to–50% incentives from the federal fund, spend over $10 billion per year on the Interstate Highway System alone.

Meanwhile, the water carriers are subsidized through river and harbor development, chiefly by the Army Corps of Engineers, currently at the rate of more than $7 billion. Like many of the freeway projects, these developments are "pork barreled" with little attention to environment or efficiency. One $2 billion water project is designed to make 450 miles of Southwestern rivers navigable into the heart of Oklahoma. Most experts believe the cost will vastly outweigh the gain, no matter how the gain is measured. But since it is costing nothing to the powerful few who gain, the project continues.

MASS TRANSIT

The collapse of a viable passenger rail system, in conjunction with highway subsidies, has led to the rise of an immense "freeway establishment." As road construction has proliferated, auto production climbed and gasoline sales increased, the automobile–gasoline lobby has attained a grip on power which finds no equal in American history. Even the much discussed military–industrial complex pales in comparison. The oil, auto, bus, and trucking industries, with powerful ties to major financial institutions, spend millions every month to influence public policy.

Lobbyists for the oil–gasoline complex work through campaign contributions, liberal loan advancements, direct payoffs (through legislators' law firms), and public relations. At a conservative estimate, one–third of all money spent for political influence in the United States comes from this bloc. Politicians elected by the oil and auto industries bear impassioned witness to their love of America, her land, her environment, and of course, her flag.

The impact includes an immense network of highways, often six– or eight–laned where four would do, traversing parallel routes, built without thought of environmental consequences or more efficient alternatives.

Urban centers receive ever-greater numbers of cars pouring into their downtown areas, which must somehow be accommodated. Communities are sliced in half by ugly freeway overpasses. Insiders reap fortunes from real estate investments along routes for new projects, despite the kickbacks they must pay to decisionmakers. Mountainsides are sliced out to make way for highways. And, of course, the air becomes more burdened with noxious chemicals, day after day.

WHAT MUST BE DONE

There *are* alternatives, and we should be developing and using them.

Really competitive transportation systems would automatically set rates according to rational criteria. Competition *within* modes would preclude excess profits and waste of transportation resources.

The optimum solution, therefore, would involve the dissolution by law of rate bureaus; divestiture of the large carriers; and strict antitrust enforcement with surveillance of management to prevent interlocking control. This would still leave us with a rail system with some monopoly power, difficult to break up with only one track or right-of-way in many areas, and with high natural economic barriers to entry of new firms. The answer to this is for the federal government to purchase, over a four or five year period at $5 or 6 billion a year, all railroad track, rights-of-way, terminals, and switching facilities. The government would then set reasonable user fees to recover the cost and maintain these facilities.

As long as monopoly power exists, close rate regulation is necessary. This means computerized analysis of rates on an ongoing basis according to statistically sophisticated procedures and through accounting checks. Maximum rate ceilings based on cost, plus a reasonable rate of return, are necessary. Of course, this is what the ICC was designed to do when it was created back in 1887. The authority is there. What is necessary is the right personnel and the will.

The primary transit system into and between cities should be railways, which are relatively non-polluting and carry a large number of passengers per unit of space.

To the extent that auto transport is necessary (particularly given the already extensive interstate highway system), modifications are possible. Steam-powered, longe-range interurban cars should be developed and made available on a rental basis, since with such limited use rental would be more economical than ownership. These vehicles would be built for safety and their speed would be limited to 75 mph. Small electrical cars, possibly coin-operated, would be distributed around cities for use by anyone, but otherwise cars would be banned from urban centers.

The internal combustion engine must be banned by law. Following the lead of a bill recently introduced in the California legislature, the federal government should offer a $500 million "reward" to any company which produces a certain number of safe, pollution-free steam or electric powered vehicles for interurban transport. The reward should be from federal gasoline tax revenues. Once this is achieved, a tax on the internal combustion engine should be assessed which will double every year with a complete ban after five or ten years.

There should be an immediate moratorium, with rare exceptions, on new freeway construction. The present Highway Trust Fund should be used to finance whatever transportation facilities are most practical or needed in any area, whether they are rapid transit systems, bicycle paths, or anything else. In any case, the federal government should give nine dollars for every dollar provided by cities for mass transit research and *construction*. All autos entering urban centers should be taxed 10 to 25 cents as an entry fee. A heavy tax should be imposed on vehicles to the degree to which they pollute, or use up rapidly diminishing resources. These revenues should be used for research into and construction of mass transit facilities, fuel substitutes, and recycling procedures.

Small, "golf cart" vehicles should be used on most streets, and bicycles should enjoy a renaissance. Pedestrian malls and parks should take the place of streets and parking lots.

Chapter 3

Air Pollution: Moving Beyond Motherhood

by John C. Esposito

All politicians are in favor of air pollution control—along with God, country, flag and motherhood. It would be folly in this day for a candidate not to nail a platitude or two on the subject into his political platform. If promises are kept general enough, air pollution control can be a low-cost political plank, running minimal risk of polarizing the electorate.

The fact is that air pollution control is not a political issue in the sense that Vietnam, race and crime are. These more volatile issues are truly political because large portions of the electorate have clearly-defined views regarding the resolution of these problems. Consequently, politicians seeking support on these issues must commit themselves to step in on one side or the other of a problem. In short, they must promise that some persons or groups will win and that others will lose. Similarly, air pollution control will become a true political issue when its constituency has developed criteria by which to determine when it has won or lost. Until that time, the environmental issue will continue to be buried by the rhetoric of instant environmentalists. What follows are some guidelines which may help determine whether your candidate for office is serious about air pollution control—or whether you're being had. I have not bothered to outline the suggestions for minor tinkering with the present air pollution control law. The suggestions to be discussed are as fundamental as the problem to be solved.

LEGISLATIVE PHASE-OUT OF THE INTERNAL COMBUSTION ENGINE

The automobile is the single largest source of air pollution. Nationally it accounts for about 60% of the problem; in many cities the figure is closer to 85%. Auto emissions are responsible for the phenomenon known as photochemical smog. Nitrogen dioxide—an automotive pollutant yet to be controlled by federal regulations—captures the sun's ultraviolet rays and interacts with another auto pollutant, unburned hydrocarbon, to form the gray–brown mist which makes city life so unpleasant and unhealthy. Another automotive emission, carbon monoxide, has been shown to have adverse health effects at levels found in almost every major city.

Automotive emissions (hydrocarbons and carbon monoxide only) have been "regulated" by federal standards since 1968. Autos sold since that time have been equipped with controls which have cost purchasers at least 1.5 billion dollars. This expenditure might be justified if the public got its money's worth. In fact, however, it has been shortchanged. Recent federal test data indicate that as many as 80% of the post–1968 cars on the road fail the federal standards. And the indications are that the auto industry is planning to charge us more for even less. Charles Heinen, Chrysler's emissions specialist, recently announced that controls for oxides of nitrogen may require a national expenditure of *ten billion dollars*. One might gauge the industry's faith in the performance of these future pollution controls by the fact that it is fighting legislative proposals to require that controls be included as part of the manufacturer's warranty.

Even if present controls can be improved and the public is willing to absorb the multi–billion dollar cost, we are engaged in nothing more than a monumentally expensive holding action. The engine used to propel automobiles sold today, the internal combustion engine is inherently dirty, depending as it does on explosion—a most inefficient means of combustion. The June 1968 report to Congress of the National Air Pollution Control Administration (which is itself overly optimisitc because it assumes that the present controls work) states:

"It should be pointed out that if more stringent national control is not imposed after 1970, vehicular pollution levels will reach a minimum during the late 1970's and then begin to rise in response to ever-expanding numbers of motor vehicles. Consequently, *the current and pro-*

posed standards do more to keep the problem from getting worse than to solve it." [Author's italics]

Immediately feasible alternatives do exist. Experts—or at least those not indentured to the auto industry—generally agree that the Rankine Cycle (or steam) engine can be mass produced within several years. The Rankin Cycle engine matches or outdoes the internal combustion engine with respect to performance, safety, cost and dependability. The internal combustion engine can *never* be cleaned up to match the present emission characteristics of the Rankine Cycle: no lead, oxides of nitrogen reduced by a factor of about 25 from the uncontrolled internal combustion engine, carbon monoxide and unburned hydrocarbons reduced to 1% of the uncontrolled internal combustion engine.

It is safe to say that the automobile industry will not voluntarily abandon the engine that made Detroit famous, whether it be in favor of the Rankine Cycle, electric, turbine or other alternative engine. There is simply too much money and psychological energy invested in the *status quo*. The recent disclosures that even the modest controls on cars being sold today do not work may have an important impact on legislators by bringing them to the realization that the present approach to "control" of emissions from automobiles perpetuates the outmoded, inefficient and lethal internal combustion engine.

Ask your candidate for federal office whether

he will vote to ban the internal combustion engine in five years. Will he vote for a 100 million dollar–a–year research program to further develop the Rankine Cycle engine and to investigate even more advanced alternative propulsion systems? Will he support an investigation of the automobile industry in order to determine why manufacturers inevitably speak with one voice when faced with the unpleasant demand that automotive technology catch up to the 1970s?

A BALANCED TRANSPORTATION SYSTEM FOR THE NATION

An adequate public response to the air pollution problem cannot be developed until we move away from the absurdly primitive methods we have chosen to move people around our nation and our cities. The nation now has about 90 million automobiles, or a separate transportation system for every two or so persons in the country. At the same time, it cannot boast of a single mass transit system which is not inconvenient, costly or dehumanizing. (Perhaps San Francisco's Bay Area Rapid Transit System will be an exception when it begins operations.) To a large extent we can thank the auto manufacturers and others who benefit from roads for this gross imbalance. Truckers, road builders, cement and asphalt manufacturers, oil companies, automobile drivers' associations and others—all of these have locked arms with the auto industry to see that more than 15 billion dollars is spent annually on highway construction. In that land of freeways, California, Governor Reagan's proposed 1971 budget contained 793 million dollars for roads and 237 thousand dollars for mass transit. It is significant to note that one highway lobbyist made in six months 1/5 the amount of money proposed in the 1971 California budget for mass transit.

The main instrumentality for perpetuating this distortion of rational priorities is the federal government's Highway Trust Fund. The Fund—the brainchild of Congressman Fallon of Maryland and the road lobby—is designed to assure that specially earmarked funds will always be available for concrete swaths. Taxes collected on gasoline, tires and automobile accessories are segregated from the general revenues for this purpose. So while about four billion dollars comes out of this Fund each year to assist in the massive job of paving over the nation, the federal government spends less than 240 million dollars (or the same amount as the General Motors advertising budget) for mass transit.

The imbalance is of course no accident. The people who profit so handsomely from roadbuilding are also threatened by mass transit. The tension between advocates of the two modes of transportation was dramatically illustrated in California several years ago when San Francisco's Bay Area Rapid Transit System (BART) found itself strapped for funds to complete its construction. The state legislature was offered several proposals to bail BART out, including a proposal to divert 150 million dollars in gasoline taxes and auto registration revenues from roadbuilding to rapid transit. The roadbuilding lobby launched an immediate attack on the proposal. The attack was successful and the highway funds were left inviolate. Money for BART would come from other sources of general revenue. The strength of the overt activities of the roadbuilding lobby in California can be understood by the following description which appeared in the *Wall Street Journal* (June 27, 1968):

> "Not surprisingly, the massive auto-freeway lobby is in the forefront of those opposing any such diversion of highway funds. The 20 lobbyists employed in the state capital by oil companies, auto makers and dealers, truckers and highway construction firms help keep legislators well informed of any money shortages that beset the state's highway programs.
>
> "This group is well funded. For example, Al Shultz, one of six oil company lobbyists, reported $53,411 in salary and expenses for just six months of last year's legislative session. In a typical month he's paid a $4,500 salary plus $4,000 for entertainment."

There is perhaps no better example of the social havoc which could be wrought by ill–conceived highway building than the (hopefully now defunct) proposal to build a Lower Manhattan Expressway. In their wisdom, planners decided to build a 1½ mile, ten–lane expressway to connect the Williamsburg Bridge directly with the Holland Tunnel. The project in its final form would have cost 150 million dollars (100 million dollars a mile), would have eradicated scores of blocks on either side of it, wiped out thousands of jobs and seriously polluted the air. Ironically, all of this was justified on the ground that it would make for a more healthy city by expediting the flow of traffic. Community resistance centered around all of the deleterious effects of the expressway, including air pollution. The City's Department of Air Resources released a report which indicated that the proposed project would increase air pollution to levels five to ten times greater than is generally considered safe. The plan was finally shelved when Mayor Lindsay, who had changed sides several times during the controversy, finally donned the white hat to vote against the proposal. But New Yorkers came close to building what might have been America's monument to its folly in transportation planning. Ill-considered highway building joins some of the most pressing problems facing urban America today: severe environmental hazards, increased urban tensions, reduced taxable land bases and the disruption of lives. Although the effects are not always planned, the causes are. The power of the highway lobby must be overcome if we are to have livable cities.

Will your candidate for state or federal office vote to dismantle trust funds which mandate that monies be spent for highways irrespective of need? Will he demand that large amounts of this money be diverted to the building of rapid transit systems available to everyone? Will he vote for legislation which requires administrators to plan comprehensive, balanced transportation systems?

AN IMMEDIATE INVESTIGATION INTO THE ENERGY COALITION

A coordinated national attack on air pollution cannot take place without a coordinated national fuels policy. Such a policy already exists on a *de facto* basis, but it is made by what might be described as the Energy Coalition: the coal industry and the railroads which service it; the oil industry; natural gas suppliers; the atomic energy industry; and the electrical utilities. The Coalition is not always monolithic in its policies, but it is bound together by a single coincidence of interest—the enormous fuels appetite of the nation's electric utilities.

The country's need for electric power has doubled every decade since 1940. On that basis, over the next thirty years the industry would have to triple its capacity to keep up with increased demands. Electric generation requires the conversion of one form of energy—generally fuels combustion—into electricity. (Hydroelectric generation will also do it, but there are not many bodies of water left for the Corps of Engineers, the Bureau of Reclamation, TVA, or private utilities to dam.) The emissions resulting from the burning of oil and coal to produce electricity (85% of electric generation) contribute about 50% of the nation's air–borne sulfur oxides and about 25% of the particulate matter. The truism that air pollution control policy is fuels policy has special relevance here. And yet, the federal government lacks the most basic information on which to build a coordinated air pollution control policy.

With the same inexorability as the summer solstice, each June brings new predictions of blackouts and brownouts resulting from overextending the capacity of many of the country's electric utilities. To a large extent this is the result of the industry's putting all its eggs in the nuclear basket. Nuclear power generation has been shown to create as many problems as it is purported to solve. The generators are unreliable and create new environmental problems which at least rival those of conventional plants. At the same time many utilities are anxious to keep costs down so that they can continue to garner the hefty returns allowed them by docile utilities commissions.

In the face of these developments, the Energy Coalition has tightened its grip of secrecy, releasing only such information as will light up its income statements. Coal operators, for instance, are so paranoic about public knowledge of their affairs that they refused to provide their own trade association with basic information regarding ownership and location of coal. ("That business is run by the best minds of the Twelfth Century,"—this comment from a *friend* of the industry.)

Will your candidate for state or federal office demand that the following questions be asked—and answered in detail? Just where are the low-sulfur coal reserves (enough to last hundreds of years) and who owns them? Why has the industry refused to open mines in low-sulfur areas? What are the true costs of oil desulfurization? (Petroleum economist S.A. Adelman claims that the industry figure for the additional costs of desulfurizing oil is inflated by 300%.) Are we faced with a possibility of a natural gas shortage? (Natural gas is one of the cleanest burning of all fuels which can be used to generate electricity.) Or are the owners of natural gas reserves keeping fuel in the ground in order to drive prices up?

A public authority—either a legislative committee or special commission—armed with full subpoena power must find the answers to these and other such questions—and find them quickly. The main paradox to be resolved is why the most fuel-rich nation on earth is unable to provide its people with adequate electric power *and* clean air.

MAXIMUM CONTROLS ON EMISSIONS FROM STATIONARY SOURCES

Electrical utilities and manufacturing are conservatively estimated to spew out about 120 billion pounds of contaminants annually, or about 600 pounds of particulates, sulfur oxides, fluorides and scores of more exotic materials for every person in the United States. Under present legislation the situation will worsen at an alarming rate. For instance, electric utilities now account for over 62 billion pounds of sulfur oxides (SO_x) annually. Projections of the current rate to 1980 promise SO_x emissions from utilities 90 billion pounds a year. Air-borne garbage from manufacturing facilities is expected to increase to almost unimaginable levels if quick action is not taken.

Congress has responded to this crisis with legislation which can best be described briefly as labyrinthine. While the details are complicated, the ineffectiveness of the law can be graphically illustrated by the following fact: As of July, 1970—nearly three years after the enactment of the Air Quality Act of 1967—not a single smokestack in the nation has reduced emissions by one ounce as a result of the present federal scheme. Congressional and administrative apologists defend the present law by arguing that such things "take a long time to crank up."

The federal effort must be shifted from exhortations to "crank up" to regulations designed to bring about maximum cleanup within the shortest period of time. National standards must be prescribed for emissions from all stationary sources of pollution. These standards should be based upon a determination by the federal government of what new controls, what changes in processes, what shifts to lower polluting fuels will produce the lowest emissions possible. Present methods for achieving clean air seem to have been developed in answer to the question, "how can we find the most indirect, complex and dilatory way of approaching the problem?" Congress has so far answered the question with great success. Beware of talk of "ambient air standards," "clean air goals" and "air quality criteria." These have been rhetorical red herrings used to disguise inactivity and diffused accountability. The legislative–administrative structure best suited for dealing with the problem is as simple as the problem: find out where the emissions come from and place direct controls on them. It may come as a surprise to some readers that this has not yet been done. Ask your candidate how he feels about maximum emission control.

FINES AND CRIMINAL PENALTIES FOR POLLUTERS

Pollution is good for business. It is what the economists call an external diseconomy—a cost of producing goods which is not borne by the producer but by the society at large. As long as there is no incentive to force the polluter to install controls, he will attempt to minimize his costs by polluting at will. The largest fine ever levied against a polluter has not exceeded 25,000 dollars, and this was a one–shot proposition. Corporate pollution will not end until emissions contaminate income statements as well as the atmosphere.

Then too there is the question of criminal penalties for corporate executives and plant managers who willfully violate air pollution laws. You can be sent to jail for stealing a car but not for producing one which pollutes. You can be sent to jail for breaking into a factory but not for building one which emits materials which disrupt the lives of your neighbors.

Is your candidate willing to impose large *daily* fines on polluters? Is he willing to send corporate executives to jail for *willful* violations of the law?

CITIZEN ATTORNEYS GENERAL

No federal or state scheme for air pollution control can ever hope to be comprehensive enough to reach every facet of the problem. Bureaucratic delays, indifference, underfunding and understaffing will no doubt assure that large numbers of people will feel unprotected by any set of regulations. Public outrage against polluters can be marshaled to provide an important adjunct to the administrative process. The need is to develop legal mechanisms to arm citizens with the tools to protect their own rights when their administrators have failed them. The most important immediate step that can be taken is a federal clean air class action law.

A class action is a civil suit where a number of plaintiffs with the same grievance band together to seek damages or injunctive relief against alleged offenders. In the past the civil suit brought by a single plaintiff has not realized its full potential. This has been because in suits brought by one person to abate pollution or to seek damages the entire social cost of the defendant's action has not been brought to the attention of the court. When all the persons affected by the activities of a polluter can be brought together in a class action, all of the social costs—including injuries to mental and physical health and ecological damage—would be before the court, enabling it to balance these costs against the costs to the polluter of purchasing control equipment.

From this point of view, then, the class action can be an effective device for demonstrating through the strength of numbers the weight of the equities on the side of environmental safety. Otherwise, faced with only one or a few plaintiffs claiming relatively small damages, the corporate polluter may say, as did one executive of the Reynolds Metals Company, "It is cheaper to pay claims than to control fluorides."

Class actions on the federal level have been hampered by serious legal technicalities which must be removed by legislative action. A candidate for federal office should be asked to take a stand on expanding the class action concept.

JOB SECURITY AND SAFETY FOR WORKERS

Persons concerned with environmental issues have often been accused—and sometimes with justification—of indifference towards some of the other pressing social problems. The environmental issue could well cause yet another division between the working classes and the middle and upper classes. The fact is that years of industrial indifference has brought us to the point where there are demands that plants shut down their operations completely. For those persons who depend upon these factories for a livelihood this is, to say the least, not much of a solution. Consequently, those who consider themselves environmentalists should forge new links to workers who may not see air pollution as the most pressing issue of the day by evidencing a sensitivity and concern for their problems. Candidates addressing themselves to the environmental issue should be asked whether they are willing to deal with the internal air pollution in many factories and other working places. Are they willing to declare it illegal to shut down a plant in order to avoid compliance with air pollution laws? Are they willing to declare it illegal to fire any worker who refuses to cooperate with or who reports a violation of the air pollution laws? Are they willing to subsidize and otherwise assist workers who may be displaced by the changing commerical patterns that may result from the environmental movement?

The wasting of our environment is a deeply-rooted pattern of our industrial society. No candidate who claims to be serious about air pollution control can promise cleanup *and* business as usual. Remember, business as usual has brought us to the point we are at today.

Chapter 4

Less Power to the People

by Garrett De Bell

As I have tried to show in *The Environmental Handbook,* the increasing use of energy inevitably results in increased environmental pollution. All power results in some form of pollution, and we have reached a point where the benefits of additional power are outweighed by its negative effects on our air and water. We would be better off using less energy per person, and having a cleaner environment.

Ending the environmental deterioration stemming from power production is not primarily a technical problem. It is a question of priorities, values, and overall policy.

Industry and the public utilities would have us believe that the great need is for more research into better techniques to reduce the pollution per unit of energy used. As one example, the amount of sulfur dioxide produced in the production of a kilowatt–hour in a coal burning plant could, theoretically, be reduced by desulfuring the fuel before burning or by better stack control devices.

The flaw in this approach is that after pollution has been limited by, say, 50% per kilowatt–hour* then when the consumption of power doubles (which it now does every decade or sooner), we're right back where we started. We have half as much pollution per kilowatt-hour, and twice as many kilowatts used, so the amount of pollution produced is the same. The air is no cleaner, and despite technical progress, nothing is any better.

Government and industry's other panacea is the promise of "clean" nuclear power. Readers who would like to go into the problem in depth should read *Perils of the Peaceful Atom,* by Curtis and Hogan (Ballantine). Their central argument is that nuclear power's safety record thus far is not impressive, that there are both long– and short–term dangers from radiation and thermal pollution, and that accidents are likely. They conclude that the dangers are too great to risk the large-scale use of nuclear energy now.

So there is only one answer: we must use less energy. It is up to the government to pass legislation that will help cut down energy consumption by both individuals and industries.

We can easily do without many of the things we use energy for today since they are harmful in themselves. Electric power mowers use

---

*The emphasis in this chapter is primarily on electricity (kilowatts) but the argument generally applies also to coal, oil and other fossil fuels that can be converted to electricity.

energy for trivial convenience, yet produce lots of noise to disturb neighbors. Substitutes would be environmentally better. On a larger scale, mass transit systems that use less energy per passenger–mile are also safer and less land-consuming than automobiles.

Restrictions on specific uses of energy for trivial or inefficient purposes would be difficult to enforce. Trying to prevent people from using electric blenders or lawn mowers would likely be an exercise in futility. Fortunately, there is a simpler approach which would encourage home owners, industry, and others to cut back on energy use. This would involve changing the rate structure.

The way things stand, users (especially industrial users) are given lower rates per unit of energy, the more they use. This is because utilities want to increase energy use so they can sell more power.

Instead, laws should require that energy be sold to industries for a flat rate, with no discounts for large users. Each home or apartment should be allowed a certain amount of power sufficient for ordinary demands (for cooking, heating, refrigerating, lighting, and so on). Government regulation should set the rate for anything within this limit at cost. For any excess consumption, the rates should rise steeply.

Such a system would not directly prohibit anyone from using more energy, so there would be no bootlegging of clandestine clothes dryers, and so on. But the rapid price increase after the basic energy allowance was surpassed would encourage people to turn off lights, skip air conditioning, and stir their own drinks.

The increased cost of energy to industrial users would encourage them to economize by using less energy. For instance, recycling of aluminum would save 16,000 KWH per ton.

There are other promising approaches to help reduce energy use. Tom Turner's suggestions for prohibiting advertising by utilities are contained in another chapter. The Sierra Club has adopted a policy to this effect. Senator Proxmire's effluent tax idea, discussed in the recycling chapter, could be extended to include air pollution from power plants. This would encourage a cutback of energy use and pollution controls at the source.

A bill to provide paid, expert advocates for the public at Public Utilities Commission rate and expansion hearings should also be passed. As things are now, the public often lacks good technical representation at hearings, while power companies can produce a parade of their own hired scientists or statisticians.

Three basic changes are needed in our control over nuclear power and the Atomic Energy Commission. The AEC is currently given the duty both to promote the use of nuclear energy and to regulate its use to protect the public safety. These two functions are incompatible. The regulating function should be in a strong agency independent of the AEC. The necessity for this can be seen in the case of Dr. John Gofman and Dr. Arthur Tamplin of the Lawrence Radiation Laboratory, financed by the AEC. The two scientists presented evidence before Congressional committees and scientific groups that the AEC's current radiation limits are 10 times too high and many cases of cancer will result if these levels are actually reached. Tamplin charged that, as a result, his research group's appropriation had been slashed from $300,000 to $25,000, and the group cut from 12 people to two. The tenfold reduction in allowable radiation limits recommended by Drs. Gofman and Tamplin should be implemented. Finally, Congress should drop the limitation it has placed on liability in nuclear accidents, and force utilities using atomic power to bear complete responsibility for accidental death or injuries. This would probably stop the development of nuclear energy, since the risks are so high that insurance costs would be prohibitive.

To sum up, we need a whole new energy policy in this society. In addition to reducing the amount of pollution per unit of power, we must reduce the amount of power consumed as well, so that we can look forward to cleaner air and a time when we don't have to continually fight to keep our few remaining wild places free of power plants and power lines.

Chapter 5

Give Pesticide Policy an Ecological Conscience

by Harrison Wellford

Government response to pesticide hazards has led to a credibility gap comparable only to the one created by official commentaries on the progress of the Vietnamese war. Consider these recent developments.

In November of 1969, the Nixon administration with great fanfare announced that DDT was being banned for house, garden and certain other uses. Thirty days later, with no fanfare, three manufacturers of DDT appealed the ban and set in motion a stately procession of hearings and delays where statutory deadlines (30 days here, 90 days there) alone can consume over 200 days. In July of 1970, the second step (of 8) in the implementation of the ban—the calling of an advisory committee of scientists to consider the evidence against DDT —has not yet taken place. In the meantime, the DDT manufacturers who appealed the ban can continue to sell DDT in business-as-usual fashion over the months and years of the administrative and legal proceedings to come.

Consider also the case of 2,4,5-T. On October 29, Lee Dubridge, Science Advisor to the President, announced that government use of 2,4, 5-T herbicide (which causes birth defects in test animals) was being banned in populated areas. In February of 1970, after the Nixon administration had garnered 3 months of praise for taking a bold step in environmental protection, the Department of Agriculture, the Department of Defense and the Food and Drug Administration announced that they were not going to comply. After lengthy and embarrassing hearings chaired by Senator Hart (D–Mich.) in April, the government reconsidered. The Surgeon General announced that 2,4,5-T was again going to be banned. By July of 1970 only 10% of 2,4,5-T sales have in fact been curtailed. Again, the lengthy administrative and legal procedure of cancellation are slowly grinding into motion. In the meantime, most uses of 2,4,5-T will continue as before the ban, including the spraying of this herbicide on blueberries and other food crops.

The pesticide credibility gap goes beyond the phenomenon of the phony ban to encompass structural flaws as well as administrative ones. It is enhanced by the fact that in the 23 years since the passage of the basic pesticide control act, the federal agency in charge of implementing it has been part of a department which is itself an enthusiastic promoter and user of pesticides. As a consequence, the Pesticide Regulation Division of the Department of Agriculture has been a step–child in its own department, reporting to congressional committees stacked with representatives of agricultural producers. More significantly, pesticide control has been a hostage of land-use patterns dictated by agricultural policy. The farm program creates incentives for farmers to engage in mono-culture, while at the same time forcing them to wring ever increased yields from a constantly diminishing land base. With this intensive use, natural controls of pests are broken down.

The predominance of the growers' interest in pesticide policy has also meant that far more attention has been given to seeing that pesticides are effective against specific pests than to preventing serious harm to human and animal populations. This imbalance of priorities is vividly demonstrated by USDA's efforts to gather reports on pesticide accidents. In 1968, of an estimated 50,000 pesticide accidents nationwide, USDA investigated 155—52 of which turned out to involve poisoning of farm animals.

The face of pesticide regulation may change radically in the next few months. In July of 1970, the Nixon administration proposed the abolition of the old pesticide regulatory structure. If approved by Congress, pesticide control will become a function of the new Environmental Control Agency.

This appears to be a bold initiative for the federal government. Executive reorganizations, however, are frequently triumphs of form over substance. The appearance of action is striking but new titles and new offices are often feeble supports of change. If the officials in the new agency still report to farm committees, if the weaknesses of the federal pesticide act endure, if the burden of proof remains stacked against the pesticide victim, if pesticides continue to be approved without an accounting of all the costs and benefits, if hazards to the human environment remain subordinated to production demand in the agricultural and chemical industry —these bold new initiatives will be surely and steadily eroded.

The following recommendations provide yardsticks against which to measure the performance of the new agency and the commitment of candidates running on environmental platforms.

STREAMLINE THE CANCELLATION PROCEDURES FOR DANGEROUS PESTICIDES

As mentioned above, the cancellation procedure for dangerous pesticides moves at a tortoise's pace. Pesticides deserve their day in court but when due process becomes so elaborate that it creates years of delay, safety considerations lose their saliency.

Cancellation should be streamlined in the following manner: within 30 days after a cancellation notice has been served, a company may request a hearing. At the hearing, convened within 60 days, any interested party may present testimony. As soon as possible after the hearing but within 60 days, a final order granting or denying registration should be issued. This reform would drastically reduce the interminable delays of pesticide control.

EXPAND EXPERIMENTAL SCREENING OF PESTICIDES TO INCLUDE DATA ON CARCINOGENIC, TERATOGENIC, AND MUTAGENIC EFFECTS

Pesticide regulators have an artificially narrow view of what factors constitute a pesticide hazard. Traditionally USDA has focused on the immediate dangers to those people who come into contact with the pesticide. The long term dangers to the environment and wildlife from residual pesticides have been neglected. Long term impact on human beings through increases in the incidence of cancer, birth defects and mutations have until very recently been largely ignored. With pesticide residues increasing in air, water, and food, testing new pesticides and old ones already on the market for long term effects becomes increasingly urgent.

ESTABLISH A "PREVENTIVE DETENTION" RULE FOR PESTICIDES FOUND POTENTIALLY DANGEROUS TO PERSONS OR THE ENVIRONMENT

Under present law as interpreted by the Secretary of Agriculture, USDA cannot summarily bán the use of a pesticide unless it is found to be an "imminent hazard" to the public. USDA defines "imminent" to mean "something threatening to happen immediately." The bizarre consequences of the Department's etymology are illustrated in recent testimony before the Senate Subcommittee on Energy, Natural Resources, and the Environment:

MR. BECKWIT (committee counsel):
 . . . if the evidence were absolutely clear that wherever we applied 2,4,5-T to food crops [and] those crops were eaten, we stood, say, a

75 percent chance of a birth defect, do you feel that use [of 2,4,5-T] on food crops would not constitute an imminent hazard to health . . ?

DR. BYERLY (USDA official):
We do not now have authority in my opinion, not clear authority, to act in such a case.

The waiting period between application of 2,4,5-T to the crop and its consumption as food destroys the "imminence" of the hazard. USDA is contending, in effect, that a time bomb is not an "imminent hazard," and therefore it has no authority to prevent the bomb from being dropped.

An amendment should be passed to compel the Secretary of Agriculture to hold pesticides in "preventive detention" through temporary suspension when it may present a substantial danger to persons but the information available is insufficient for a definite determination of the scope of the hazard. This temporary suspension would be lifted after its makers have satisfied a burden of proof that it is safe.

This step will remove the largest single hurdle in the way of swift federal response to pesticide hazards.

ESTABLISH ECOLOGICAL CRITERIA FOR NEW PESTICIDES

Experimental screening of newly-developed pesticides is largely devoted to performance and human health—both considered narrowly. Performance means the effectiveness of the pesticide in killing a target pest with no attention to the impact of the poison on the total insect community. Under present federal regulations, a pesticide like Azodrin, for example, is considered effective even when it leads to a decrease in crop yield. Treatment of cotton fields with Azodrin would kill the first crop of bollworms but it would devastate also insect predators and parasites. Succeeding waves of insects, including bollworms, and entirely new pests previously under control, would find the fields clean of natural enemies and do extensive damage.

Thorough ecological research on new pesticides can no longer be postponed. The DDT case is an example of the hazards to life of whole species which may develop when health is narrowly construed.

ASSIGN EXPERIMENTAL SCREENING OF NEW PESTICIDES TO LABORATORIES INDEPENDENT OF INDUSTRY INFLUENCE

Few people realize the extent to which analysis of pesticide chemicals has become a close system for insiders only. Biological testing of these chemicals to anticipate the consequences of human exposure is neither impartial nor necessarily competent. This testing is performed through confidential contracts between the manufacturers and commercial testing laboratories. The possibilities, indeed the incentives, for abuse are obvious. As one USDA staffer recently told us, "The manufacturer runs the tests he wants to run, selects the test results which are most favorable to him and sends them to us. Rarely, if ever, will USDA ask him to submit additional data." Under the present system, a pesticide company has a clear incentive to avoid a laboratory which is embarrassingly thorough in its tests.

This initial testing is not open to independent scrutiny. Furthermore no independent tests are performed by USDA when the pesticide is presented for registration. Registration, is, in effect, a paper procedure which largely accepts at face value data submitted by the manufacturer as to the safety and effectiveness of a product.

The direct connection between the pesticide industry and the testing labs must be broken. Companies which need to satisfy ecological, human safety, and performance criteria for a proposed pesticide should submit their requests to the Environmental Control Agency. The ECA would then assign the experimental screening to certified labs on the basis of low bids. The test data would be sent directly to the agency, without prior approval from the company. The company would continue to pay for the testing of new products.

ESTABLISH PRINCIPLES OF FREEDOM OF INFORMATION FOR PESTICIDE REGULATION AND RESEARCH

It is time to dispel the secrecy which has shrouded pesticide regulation and research. The mysterious attempts by federal officials to suppress the Bionetics Report which revealed the teratogenic (birth defect causing) potential of 2,4,5-T herbicides illustrates this problem. As early as the fall of 1966, the Bionetics Laboratory, in a contract report to the National Cancer Institute, disclosed test results which showed that 2,4,5-T caused birth defects in mice. These results were concealed from other teratologists and the rest of the scientific community for three years. In this time, no action was taken by the government to minimize human exposure. Only in August of 1969 was the report pried loose for use by the teratogenicity panel of the Mrak Commission. Unfortunately the treatment of the Bionetics Reports was not an isolated case.

As a general rule, data on the toxicology, efficacy, chemical identity and epidemiology of these chemicals has never been collected, disseminated or stored in ways which allow for rapid and easy access by interested scientists or the general public. It is imperative that data on herbicides and on all pesticides which relate to the safety of the public and environmental quality be a matter of open record. In the meantime, there is no way for an individual citizen, an interested scientist, or even a member of Congress to review safety data submitted by a manufacturer either before or after a pesticide enters the market.

ESTABLISH LEGAL REMEDIES INCLUDING CLASS ACTIONS, RIGHTS OF ACTION BY INDIVIDUALS, AND CRIMINAL PENALTIES TO RESTRAIN CORPORATIONS, GOVERNMENT AGENCIES AND INDIVIDUALS FROM MISUSING PESTICIDES

The powerlessness of the individual to act when he observes or is harmed by pesticide abuses is a common theme for environmentalists. The dearth of legal remedies in this field has long undermined individual initiatives to protect the environment. Suppose for example that your neighbor insists on spraying his lawn with 2,4,5-T herbicide after it has been banned for home use. Unfortunately, he is breaking no law. Similarly, a farmer who buys 2,4,5-T for use on his pastures but then ignores a federal ban by spraying it on ditchbanks violates no law. Suppose that as an individual consumer, you are concerned about mercury residues in the flour, eggs or apples you eat. In the past, if you sued the FDA to enforce its no-residue rule for mercury, and USDA to ban the use of mercury pesticides, the Government could successfully argue that you have no "standing" in court because you suffered no damage to a "legally protected interest."

Legislation is now pending which will open the court room door to aggrieved environmentalists and consumers. The *Consumer Class Action Bill,* if passed, will allow groups of consumers, injured or cheated by specific products, to seek remedies for themselves and all other citizens in their "class." Senators Hart (D–Mich.) and McGovern (D–S. Dak.) *are sponsoring an environmental class action bill* which will give individuals the right to go to court against any public agency or private industry they believe is damaging the environment. *Senators Nelson (D–Wisc.) and Hart (D–Mich.) are promoting legislation which pro-*

vides civil and criminal penalties against individuals guilty of using pesticides in an unsafe manner.

These legal remedies promise to give environmentalists their day in court. The breakthrough for citizen action in these bills is that they relieve one of the burden of proving that he has suffered concrete harm to his personal property. More significant, they will stimulate local groups to take the initiative in curbing misuse of pesticides without waiting for government agencies to act. Their passage requires the support of candidates running on an environmental platform.

ESTABLISH A CORPS OF PESTICIDE CONTROL ADVISORS TO HELP FARMERS ESCAPE THE PESTICIDE TREADMILL

The key to control of pesticides within ecological tolerances is finding some means of monitoring and limiting their use on agricultural land. In this effort the farmer and the environmentalist are natural allies. For paradoxically the farmer, so often the scapegoat of pesticide critics, is in fact the greatest victim of pesticide abuse. Careless use of pesticides not only harms his health but increases his cost of production and may, through unplanned side effects, increase insect damage by killing valuable insect predators and parasites. Many farmers find themselves on a treadmill, using more and more chemicals to control pests which increase annually in number and variety.

Imagine the plight of the farmer who becomes worried about insect damage to his crops. He may have seen a suspicious insect in his fields or he may have heard of losses on neighboring farms. He is unsure of the nature of the insect, the extent of its infestation, the potential damage it can cause, or the methods to control it. He needs expert advice to diagnose his problem and prescribe a cure. Often the only experts available are the salesmen and field representatives of chemical and agroservice companies—"experts" who have a vested interest in confirming the farmer's worst fears.

The fieldman from Shell or Dow, urged on by bonuses, commissions, and other incentives to make sales, serves as "diagnostician, therapist, and pill dispenser"[1] for the farmer. But while the pesticides he prescribes have extremely complex ecological consequences, he is neither licensed nor required by law to demonstrate any professional qualifications. The grower, often operating on a narrow profit margin and congenitally anxious about his crops, is easy prey for these pesticide merchandisers. Robert Van Den Bosch, professor of Entomology at the University of California at Berkeley, describes this situation as "one of the major causes of excess pesticide use and associated pesticide pollution."[2]

If this exploitation of the farmer and the

---

[1] Robert Van Den Bosch, "Pesticides: Prescribing for the Ecosystem," *Environment* Magazine, April, 1970, p. 22.

[2] Ibid., p. 23.

ecological chaos it entails is to stop, growers must be provided independent and professional advice on pesticide use. Many agricultural extension workers have abdicated this responsibility. Trained in agricultural colleges in departments focused on chemical technology, they often share the company outlook and are as careless enthusiasts for pesticides as the company fieldmen.

BY PRESCRIPTION ONLY

This bondage of the manipulatable farmer to the company salesman can be broken if the following proposal is adopted in the next Congress: Farmers facing a pest problem will be required to consult with a licensed pest control adviser who will examine his fields, recommend controls *if necessary,* and keep ecological hazards to a minimum. *The farmer could buy a specific pesticide only with a prescription from his pesticide control adviser.*

Qualifications for the advisers can be determined by the Environmental Control Agency, but the farmer would have to pay for the service—at a fraction of the cost of the pesticides he formerly wasted. The pesticide control adviser would be required by law to consider biological controls and other alternatives to chemicals and to justify in writing his selection of control techniques.

The corps of pest control advisers would provide career alternatives to entomologists and other professionals in the agricultural sciences who must now choose between working for the government or industry. They could become the conscience of their profession, operating under a code of ethics emphasizing responsibility for ecological safety. If initially there are not enough private pest control advisers available, a federal corps paralleling but independent of the Federal Extension Service, might be established by the Environmental Control Agency.

This proposal is a vital step in eliminating incentives for needless pesticide use in this country.

ESTABLISH A FEDERAL CROP INSURANCE PROGRAM TO ALLOW FARMERS TO ESTABLISH PESTICIDE-FREE ZONES WITHOUT EXCESSIVE RISK

Experimentation with alternatives to chemical control of pests is stifled by the harsh economics of farming. Most farmers cannot afford the loss of even a single crop to insect pests without being financially pressed. They are therefore in no mood to take chances. With an insurance cushion, however, the farmer might be willing to experiment with biological controls. In areas where annual losses to insects are sporadic and limited in effect, he might be persuaded to establish pesticide-free zones if the insurance protected him from a sudden unexpected onslaught of insect pests.

This plan would eliminate much panic spraying by overwrought farmers. There would be no incentive to engage in wasteful programs such as prophylactic programed spraying according to fixed schedules "just in case." To avoid the problem of false claims, insect damage would be verified by a pest control adviser or his equivalent.

CUT OFF FARM SUBSIDIES TO GROWERS WHO VIOLATE HEALTH, SANITATION AND PESTICIDE SAFETY STANDARDS FOR FARM WORKERS

On October 8, 1969, in the King City area of California, employees of United Fruit were loading lettuce on trucks. Because they were paid on a piece-rate basis they worked hurriedly, for any pause was their economic loss. The nearest toilet was 60 minutes (round-trip) away. As the day wore on, one worker was observed urinating on the lettuce. On the same day, in Monterey County, a six man crew was pulling a carrot-picking machine of Bob Sanders Carrot Company. They had been working since 6:30 A.M. without toilet, handwashing or drinking water facilities. The field was their restroom. A pile of fresh human feces and toilet paper lay in the line of carrots waiting to be picked up by the machine (information from Farm Workers Affidavit cited in petition to the Secretary of Agriculture by the Association of California Consumers et. al., July 27, 1970). These commodities, packaged in the fields, are frequently sent directly to supermarkets and other retail outlets.

The workers have no choice. They work long hours, surrounded by acres of celery, lettuce, tomatoes, carrots and artichokes, far from any home, gas station, or any area where crops are not growing. They cannot use the highway. If they use an irrigation ditch, crops become contaminated when irrigated. Some refuse to relieve themselves in the fields, but they become ill trying to control themselves for an entire eight to twelve hour day. Furthermore, many employers make it clear that farm workers need no toilet and are expected to use the surrounding area.

These attitudes are indicative of some growers' indifference to the health problems of farm workers and sanitation of the food they market. Safety standards for pesticide use, like sanitation laws, are widely and flagrantly violated by large growers from California and Florida. The list of violations is tedious to relate: farm workers in contact with pesticides have no place to wash their hands; recently sprayed fields are not posted; waiting periods after spraying are not observed; medical care is not available. Violations of these standards threaten the health of the farm workers and the contamination of the foodstuffs they harvest.

The United States Department of Agriculture delivers huge subsidies to growers who regularly violate health and sanitation laws. On July 27, 1970, the California Rural Legal Association petitioned the USDA to cut off payments to thirty agricultural growers who received agricultural subsidies of $7,100,000 in 1969 when in flagrant violation of these laws. One alleged violator, J. G. Boswell, received subsidies of $4,370,657 in 1969, the largest single beneficiary of the farm program in the nation. J. G. Boswell sits on the board of Safeway Stores which buys many of his fruits and vegetables. These foodstuffs are frequently packaged in the fields and therefore sold to Safeways' customers in the same condition in which they are picked.

Many of these violations are reported by local health officials, but little enforcement activity follows. The proposal stated above which would require an amendment to farm subsidy legislation would force USDA to cut off farm subsidies to growers who have been found in violation of health and safety standards. There is a precedent in the Sugar Act which compels USDA to cut off subsidies to farmers who violate child–labor and minimum wage regulations. In this proposal, subsidies should include agricultural conservation program payments as well as crop limitation payments. With this law enforced, it would be a simple matter for USDA to require all the subsidy applicants to present evidence of compliance with health, sanitation and safety laws before agricultural subsidies are paid.

These proposals are fundamental to an ecologically sound pesticide policy. They provide a platform for practical environmental action upon which candidates can be asked to stand. Ideally a coalition of farmers and environmentalists should be formed to advocate these policies. Many of these reforms are included in amendments to the Federal Insecticide, Fungicide and Rodenticide Act sponsored by Senator Hart of Michigan and Senator Nelson of Wisconsin. Bills encompassing these amendments are likely to be pending in Congress by September 1970.

Chapter 6

A Bill of Rights for Wildlife

by Joan McIntyre

Architect Zach Stewart once startled a group of lawyers interested in environmental law by stating that the concept of one man—one vote should include eagles and salamanders. The lawyers did not understand. They thought the idea charming but did not see it as serious or possible. Yet if we are to develop an effective legislative approach to wildlife we must first review our assumptions about other creatures, and we should next review our vision. Both are essential to our direction and our goal.

"BAD" ANIMALS AND "GOOD" ANIMALS

We are used to thinking of what value other animals have for us. In this sense, "value" is most often economic. We assume that domestic animals have intrinsic value, and if threatened by wild ones, the choice to us is clear. There were some wonderful handbooks published by the U.S. Department of Agriculture in the '20s which described various pests and assigned to them a host of mythical and disgusting characteristics. Birds and mammals stole corn and grain, were crafty and vicious, stupid and cruel. Wild animals that preyed on favored game animals were singled out for special attack. The bluejay who raided nests was a criminal, the mountain lion who ate a deer was bloodthirsty. By and large, we operate on this same philosophy today, and it determines our basic approach to wildlife conservation.

We do tend to protect our "good" animals. A deer is a good animal for a hunter; a fox, in keeping down the rodent population, may be a good animal for a farmer (if the fox doesn't kill chickens); and a beaver may (in developing trout habitat) be a good animal for a fisherman. Then there are all of the good animals we can kill, eat, wear, capture, look at, or experiment with. Recently we have come a step further and started to see all wildlife as having value in keeping the machinery of the ecological community well oiled and functional. But this is still a man-serving view of wildlife. Let's not kill off the last tiger or kit fox or pup fish, because we may find out that they were the essential cotter pin in the nature machine, and without them the whole works may fall apart. Our enlightened ecological approach to wildlife now sees creatures as part of the machinery, and we need to keep the machinery going for our benefit. And so we have the strange victory of endangered species legislation and think if we can keep some magical number of animals alive here and there we have fulfilled our compact with "nature and nature's god."

But what about one man—one vote, or one timber wolf—one vote?

I would suggest, along with Mr. Stewart and others, that wildlife has its own intrinsic right to be: to exist in the world, to pursue its own destiny and follow the path of its own evolution. And I would further suggest that any meaningful legislative program must be constructed on a new morality, must be directed at achieving a Bill of Rights for all wild creatures, everywhere.

Clearly there are problems. There is fierce competition among all of us for space, for resources, for the little room left under the sun. But just as we strain for a social order which grants humans their right to life, liberty and the pursuit of happiness, so must we strain for an ecological order which extends these essential rights to all living creatures.

THE "LIST"

We have presently some token federal legislation that protects a few non-native species by banning their import into the United States. This widely hailed Endangered Species Conservation Act is deficient in detail and in intent. It covers only subspecies in particular locations and not throughout their range. It bans the import of leopards from Formosa while allowing the import of leopards from Somali. The Act does not in any way protect resident wildlife already named as endangered by the U.S. Department of Interior. You can still hunt endangered timber wolves in Minnesota or trap endangered kit foxes in the San Joaquin Valley. But probably the most serious shortcoming of the Act is the concept of the endangered species list.

The list is the live—or—die roster of wild animals. An animal on the list may turn out to be lucky. Animals not on the list may have been left off for the simple reason that no one bothered to study their situation sufficiently to determine if it is serious enough to include them. Noel Simon, formerly of the International Union for the Conservation of Nature, noted in a private memo, "It seems probable that within the next few decades a number of forms currently regarded as common could disappear *before anyone was aware that a problem existed.*"

The existence of the list promotes a false sense of security and makes it possible to exploit and kill wildlife for fun and profit with righteous abandon. If an animal is not on the list, so the reasoning goes, then it isn't endangered and it's perfectly all right to go out and kill it; or in the sweet terminology of the 70's, to "harvest" it. Those who make money killing wildlife always assure us that in "harvesting the surplus" they are actually doing nature's work, since if they didn't kill animals the animals would die. The eco—pornography of the skin and hide trade is as earnest as that of the power companies, and just as specious. The way a wildlife population stabilizes itself in its habitat is the business of the population and the habitat, and should not be interpreted by someone who wants to make a fast buck with the numbers game. The harvest, moreover, is customarily of trophy animals—perhaps the fittest for survival in their environment but especially vulnerable simply because their heads will look good on a wall. Further, hunters are not traditionally likely to go far from highways, so their alleged protection of the environment from overbrowsing is at best localized in any event. One man's "surplus," and the sex-symbol drive to eradicate it, is another man's wilderness.

ALL WILDLIFE IS ENDANGERED

We need to change our vocabulary in framing new legislation. We must forget the idea of surplus. There are no surplus wild animals anywhere in the world. Loss of habitat, pollution, control programs, the human population explosion, over-hunting and the skin trade threaten wildlife everywhere. Unless stringent measures are taken soon, we will, by default, succeed in wiping out most of the wild animals in the world within the next few decades. At best we will be left with some collectors' populations; small unnatural ecological zoos to assuage our guilt and bring in tourist dollars. And we will also have some large populations of heavily managed animals that we will submit to the annual slaughter called harvesting. But diverse wildlife populations inhabiting their rightful share of the planet will be gone.

Let us shift the burden of proof to those who wish to exploit and kill wild animals. It should be up to them, from now on, to prove conclusively that there are lasting moral and scientific reasons for killing any wild creatures for any purpose whatsoever. If, because of our tampering with ecosystems, serious problems occur, then any management should be done with the aim to encourage diversity and maintain the ecological order. Even that is tricky and requires administration by dedicated and wise earth housekeepers (as envisioned by Gary Snyder), not by narrowly professional game-crop salesmen.

RESTRICT IMPORTS

We need immediate and effective legislation against the importation and sale of any wild animal product that requires the death of the animal. Let us remove wild animals from the market place. We can find adequate and inexpensive substitutes for wild fur coats, snakeskin belts and sealskin boots. If we must keep pets, we can entertain ourselves with domestic animals, not condemn wild creatures to the lingering death of captivity and overlove. We should take a good look at the sacred cow of scientific research and reassess how much of it is scientific and how much of it is busy work. Vervet monkeys were once common in East Africa. Now they are common in laboratories and rare in East Africa. Zoos, as suggested by Desmond Morris, would be much more valuable if they provided suitable environments for the animals they have, rather than compulsively collecting new ones. Wild animals are interesting because their behavior is interesting: if we have to view them it would be better for them and for us if they have an environment that would allow them to be something of their natural selves.

LIMIT STATE AUTHORITY

Almost all of the resident wildlife of the United States is administered and regulated by state Departments of Fish and Game or Wildlife Conservation, whose primary purpose is to assure a stock of huntable and capturable animals for the 18 million sportsmen who spend an estimated one billion dollars annually in the pursuit and killing of wildlife. The states have a traditional and possibly untested legal claim to all native species. The Bald Eagle is the only animal in the country protected by federal law, a somewhat hollow honor for a bird being destroyed by dieldrin poisoning. No other creature, however rare or magnificent, is protected by national law. And it is the hunter, livestock keeper or farmer, who most often controls the nature of state wildlife legislation. This is particularly serious in the western states and Alaska, where hunting and fishing are big business, and where legislators are particularly susceptible to the lobbying of sportsmen. It is necessary to take the management of wildlife out of the exclusive control of fishing and hunting oriented agencies and put it into the hands of those whose primary responsibility is toward maintaining ecological diversity.

PROTECTING WILDERNESS

Wildlife and wilderness are interdependent and mutually protective. When the wild animals are gone it is easier to develop an area. What makes a place priceless, very often, is its wildlife populations. And by protecting the habitat we protect the animals. There is enormous, persistent pressure these days on the part of state agencies to allow hunting in the national parks. We need laws that would clearly and forever put national parks and other public wilderness out of the reach of hunters. Imagine a "wilderness experience" consisting of dodging weekend deer hunters! We still accept the bizarre notion that it's okay to hunt on a wildlife refuge, and the Department of the Interior calmly assures us that such a policy "fulfills two important functions: (1) a balancing of animals with available habitat (2) recreation for the sportsman."

We should set our sights toward increasing the amount of available habitat, not toward finding ways to balance animals with what's available. There is too little habitat left already.

TERRITORY VS. BOUNDARY

Animals and birds do not understand political boundaries. They can probably teach us a lot about territory, but they have a tendency to ignore state and national lines. We need effective national legislation that recognizes the migratory and nomadic nature of many wild birds and mammals, and which protects them wherever found. We should lead the way in instituting international agreements protecting migratory wildlife, with particular emphasis on marine life.

PREDATORS

The situation with regard to predatory mammals is grave. Creatures that are not killed by predator control programs are hunted as varmints or bountied as pests. We need to press for state and federal legislation to remove bounties; to reestablish and reintroduce natural predators into national parks and wilderness areas; and to eliminate all state and federal predator control programs. We need a program of protection for all predatory animals in the United States, including owls, hawks, eagles and ravens. Seals, sea lions and otters also need protection as predatory marine mammals to prevent their decimation by commercial fishermen.

PENDING LEGISLATION

There is some specific legislation in the U.S. Congress that should be supported. Senator Allan Cranston (D–Calif.) has introduced a bill that would extend the protection of the Endangered Species Conservation Act to resident endangered wildlife, and take the control of that wildlife out of the hands of the state agencies. The bill, S. 3888, will be vigorously opposed and needs lots of support for passage. A bill introduced by Congressman John Saylor (R–Pa.) would prohibit the killing of any wild animal from an aircraft (H. 1518 A). A number of bills would ban the use of DDT. The celebrated Department of Agriculture ban turns out to be only a change of labels. The label now says you can't use DDT near aquatic areas, etc., but you can still buy and use DDT wherever you want, if you forget to read the label. Effective legislation stopping the use of DDT and other long-lived chlorinated hydrocarbons is essential for the preservation of many species of birds and mammals.

A number of bills have been introduced in the House to establish a national policy with regard to predatory mammals. Authored by John Saylor (R–Penn.) (H. 11425); Sylvio Conte (R–Mass.) (11405), Martha Griffiths (D–Mich.) (11454), and Ogden Reid (R–New York.) (11236), this legislation would declare wild predatory mammals a national wildlife resource, prohibit the use of poisons for predator control, and limit the number of mammal control agents that can be employed by the federal government. These bills have been referred to the Subcommittee on Fisheries and Wildlife Conservation (Chair. Dingell, D–Mich.) and hearings should be requested before this Congress dies and the bills die with it.

But not only do we need specific and effective programs—we also need vision. Somehow we must transcend our time and place and get the perspective of evolution flowing through our veins. Five hundred years ago the idea of human rights was unthinkable to most. Today the idea of wildlife rights may seem outrageous—and, to some, incomprehensible. But we can't get anywhere without beginning. One of the very best things Aldo Leopold said was:

"Only a mountain has lived long enough to listen objectively to the howl of a wolf."

Maybe we should let the mountain manage the wolf for a while, and declare the rights of all wild animals to be self-evident and equal.

Chapter 7

Wilderness

by Harvey Manning

Kenneth Brower's chapter on "Wilderness" in *The Environmental Handbook* is a fine practical and personal rationale for the preservation of wilderness areas in America and the rest of the world. Many of the same assumptions that move people like the Browers have led legislators to make laws for the protection of America's wilderness. Some of these laws are entirely adequate to the needs, but are not properly implemented; others are inadequate or lacking. New laws must be written in several areas of wilderness legislation. The following proposals are presented as a program designed to enlarge and protect the existing wilderness system of wildlands:

I. CITIZEN PRESSURE MUST BE PLACED ON FEDERAL AGENCIES AND THE CONGRESS TO FORCE THEM TO PROPERLY IMPLEMENT THE WILDERNESS ACT.

The Wilderness Act of 1964 placed 54 areas of federal lands in the national wilderness system. It also directed that by 1974 34 national forest primitive areas and all substantial roadless areas of national parks and national wildlife refuges should be studied as potential wilderness areas.

It has been six years since the Wilderness Act was passed; the deadline for completing studies of these important areas is approaching; and the job is scarcely under way. Congress has put six of the primitive areas (with additional bordering lands) in wilderness, leaving 28 to act on. The Forest Service has submitted seven additional proposals to Congress and plans to complete its review of the other 21 areas before 1974. However, in virtually every case the Forest Service has proposed that wilderness areas be much smaller than conservationists suggested.

The Fish and Wildlife Service has reviewed 27 wildlife refuges, and wilderness proposals for these are now before Congress. Studies of the remaining 55 refuges, among them the enormous, magnificent, and coveted lands of Alaska, are expected to be finished by 1974. Some of the resulting proposals are certain to be highly controversial.

The National Park Service seems to have decided to ignore the Wilderness Act, so court action may be necessary to force compliance with the law. Only three wilderness proposals have been submitted to Congress by the Park Service. Hearings have been held on 11 others, but no subsequent proposals have been forwarded to Congress. The rest of the national park system remains in limbo.

Congress is also failing to maintain a proper schedule of wilderness activity. The Senate Interior Committee, chaired by Senator Henry Jackson, an original proponent of the Wilderness Bill, is proceeding deliberately, but the House Interior Committee, chaired by Wayne Aspinall, who gutted the Wilderness Act after sitting on it for years, is now bottling up bills passed by the Senate.

A major citizen effort is urgently required to fulfill the intent of the Wilderness Act.

We must:

(1) insist that the National Park Service obey the law and complete studies of all areas covered by the Wilderness Act for inclusion in the Wilderness System;

(2) convince the three federal agencies to prepare meaningful, rather than token, wilderness proposals; and

(3) demand that Congress take action on pending proposals and seek necessary improvements on existing wilderness legislation.

II. THE U. S. FOREST SERVICE AND THE NATIONAL PARK SERVICE MUST STOP EVADING THE INTENT OF THE WILDERNESS ACT OF 1964.

A central purpose of the Wilderness Act was to restrict the administrative freedom of the U.S. Forest Service and the National Park Service. Bureaucrats in these organizations, however, are dragging their feet in the hope of minimizing the national wilderness system. By adopting an extremely strict interpretation of the Wilderness Act, they are attempting to define wilderness out of existence.

One ploy of the National Park Service is the "threshold zone." The NPS maintains that the edge of a road is not wild, and, therefore, a wilderness boundary should be pushed back from the road 1/8, 1, or even 2 miles. This argument is used to justify small wilderness areas with large thresholds, which the NPS could later use for more development of roads and hotels.

Another dangerous Park Service concept is the notion of "enclaves" deep in the wilderness. For example, the preliminary wilderness proposal for the North Cascades National Park is riddled with dozens of 1/8-mile circles of non-wilderness for toilets and scientific instruments as well as back country hostels complete with restaurants and cozy bunks. An earlier version of the proposal even had enclaves for heliports on high alpine ridges!

An interesting example of Park Service

double-talk is the notion of "motor vehicle trails," 12-foot-wide roads designed for low-speed driving, presumably with car windows open to let sounds and smells of nature penetrate the vehicle interior. To allow for this variety of "wilderness experience by automobile" the Park Service wants to exclude large areas of land from protection of the Wilderness Act.

Purists of the U.S. Forest Service are at once sophisticated and crude. They argue persuasively that lonesomeness is essential to wilderness and that any popular area isn't really wild. Therefore, they want to reserve the wilderness designation for remote and rugged lands, while calling heavily-traveled country "roadless areas." Motorcycles would even be allowed in these areas. The clear intent of such obfuscation is keeping as much land as possible in bureaucratic hands without interference from Congress and the Wilderness Act.

III. CONGRESS MUST TAKE IMMEDIATE ACTION TO STRENGTHEN THE WILDERNESS ACT.

The Wilderness Act passed by Congress in 1964 was a sad remnant of the Wilderness Bill introduced in 1956. Led by Representative Wayne Aspinall, chairman of the House Interior Committee, the mining lobby then occupied (and still does) the Congressional "narrows." For years Aspinall and his supporters blocked consideration of the bill, repeatedly passed by the Senate, and only released it to the floor of the House after wilderness supporters reluctantly gave in to their demands.

Under terms of the Act, mineral claims may be located in wilderness areas until 1984, and exploited indefinitely thereafter. Obviously, long before then the miners will have inspected every wilderness area foot by foot and staked out much of it. Obviously, no part of the national wilderness system which contains even the most meager mineral deposits is genuinely protected.

Surely, the national interest requires an inventory of mineral resources—but let the prospecting be done by the U.S. Geological Survey. If in some distant future certain deposits are needed by the nation, let the Congress of 1990 or 2040 decide each case on its merits. For now we must lock exploiters out of the wilderness areas and lock them out for good. The minerals will not go away.

The Wilderness Act also must be amended to evict sheep and cattle. Some Forest Service officers would like to train Americans to enjoy scenes of domestic animals wandering about mountain gardens in an Alpine manner, but the resulting cow pies and wallows do not improve highland streams and lakes. John Muir put it well: "As sheep advance, flowers, vegetation, grass, soil, plenty and poetry vanish."

IV. THE MINING LAW MUST BE RADICALLY REVISED AND MADE PART OF A NEW PUBLIC LAND POLICY THAT CONSIDERS ALL LAND RESOURCES.

At present, miners have free run of national forests, including wilderness areas, and even retain rights in national monuments and some national parks. To continue the frontier land policy of the past this late in the 20th century is wicked folly.

Congress must adopt new legislation which puts minerals on an equal status with other resources, such as timber and recreation, and gives the administration agency full supervision over prospecting and mining. The "finders-keepers" philosophy must be replaced by a recognition that the people of the nation own the minerals on public lands, as they do the trees; private parties should be allowed to extract minerals only on a leasing basis, and only if they can preserve other resources in the course of mining public lands.

New mining laws must wipe from the books all existing claims on public lands by recognizing only those equities holders of these claims may have established by actual expenditures of time and money. The law must take into account that as a result of the 1872 law, the mining industry is pervaded by a basic dishonesty, and many existing mineral claims are fraudulent. This is because the law does not require proof of mineral value, offering miners an incentive to stake claims where substantive value is doubtful.

V. DE FACTO WILDLANDS LACKING STATUTORY PROTECTION MUST BE ADDED TO THE WILDERNESS SYSTEM. AN END TO ROAD-BUILDING MUST BE SOUGHT IN AREAS UNDER CONSIDERATION.

Many *de facto* wildlands, including some of the finest potential elements of the wilderness system, were not placed in a primitive area, wildlife refuge or national park, and are thus omitted from the review process of the Wilderness Act. Conservationists have, to date, succeeded in bringing before Congress seven wilderness proposals covering *de facto* wildlands. This is only a bare beginning.

Any person who knows of or lives near a *de facto* wildland which needs protection, but is not yet being considered by Congress, should work to develop a proposal. If no local group exists to initiate the campaign, one should be assembled specifically for the purpose. The local group should solicit the help of national organizations.

The first step is to draw boundaries. At the start of such an effort fine detail and Forest Service "expert knowledge" are not very helpful. The next step is publicizing the proposal locally and among national conservation groups. Third comes introduction of a bill into

Congress through the agency of a sympathetic Congressman or Senator, at the same time asking Congressmen to put pressure on the Forest Service for a moratorium on road-building and resource extraction.

VI. MANY PUBLIC LAND GRANTS OF THE PAST MUST BE CONSIDERED PRESENTLY HELD BY "SECOND CLASS OWNERSHIP."

Throughout the West are countless thousands of "patented" mining claims which have been fully transferred into private ownership under the terms of the 1872 laws. Many of these lands are within national parks and wilderness areas. Few have any real mineral values, but all have blackmail value. Public agencies are attempting to purchase certain of these lands, but the prices are grossly inflated by the areas' potential for recreational subdivision and the huge value placed on such lands by lovers of unspoiled wilderness.

In addition to mining patents, vast empires of the West were given away to assist the railroads by ignorant, or corrupt Congresses in the 19th century. The Northern Pacific alone was handed 40,000,000 acres. Federal grants to all railroads amounted to 181,000,000 acres, or 282,813 square miles—an area larger than Washington, Oregon, and Idaho combined. Fully 22 percent of what was to become the State of Washington was given to the railroads, principally the Northern Pacific. Very small amounts of this land ever had any part in assisting construction of railroads, and to the present time most railroad territory has not been touched. Much of this land represents a total investment by the current owner, over a century or more, of only a few dollars an acre.

Congress must declare as a bold new policy that tainted ownership is second-class ownership: if the land was taken improperly, the title is not clear. Such a policy would allow stolen lands to be taken back into the public domain at fair prices.

VII. SEVERAL CATEGORIES OF WILDNESS, RANGING FROM "CLOSE-TO-HOME" TO "SUPER-WILD," MUST BE RECOGNIZED.

Wilderness defenders must broaden their goals by supporting a zoning and land acquisition system along the following lines:

Zone 1—City and Suburb. Begin with urban and suburban parks—containing natural areas with trails—located minutes from the homes of the millions of urban dwellers.

Zone 2—Near–the–City Natural Areas. Within an approximately 1-2 hour drive or bus ride from central city, there should be intensive development of campgrounds and trails, as opportunities exist. Most people seeking outdoor recreation do not want to spend half a day traveling to far places; they take the closest opportunity. Providing near-city camping and hiking not only serves most urban dwellers, but relieves population pressure on more remote lands, including wilderness.

Zone 3—Multiple-Use Areas. Overlapping Zone 2 is the region where commodity extraction (such as logging) and recreation co-exist. Two changes in public—especially Forest Service—policy are needed here. First, the excessive building of permanent roads and the accompaning destruction of trails must be halted; many present roads should be abandoned. Second, trailbikes and other machines must be barred from all trails everywhere. It is argued that trailbike riders enjoy their sport; the same may be said for arsonists. Both these measures—the restricting of road building to keep cars out and the banning of machines from trails—would enlarge the domain of quiet to provide a wilderness-like experience in areas principally devoted to such use as logging.

Zone 4—Wilderness Fringes. On the outer edges of large, true wilderness areas protected by the Wilderness Act, it may often be appropriate and desirable to build large numbers of trails to high standards. By means of intensive trail development of the fringes, the interior can be kept wilder under full protection of the Wilderness Act.

Zone 5—Wilderness Cores. By contrast with the fringes, the wilderness cores should have a very minimum number of high-standard trunk trails. Other trails should be low-standard and mainly should be allowed to "happen"—made by boots over the years.

In the Washington Cascades, the U.S. Forest Service is proceeding in exactly the wrong direction. It is building too many roads in multiple-use areas, obliterating existing trails and not replacing them. In wilderness cores, it is building too many trails too elaborately—super-trails with ridiculously-flat 10 per cent grades, a three foot wide tread, and a "preventative maintenance" swath of 50–100 feet where trees are cut down to prevent them from some day falling down and blocking the trail. By these means the Forest Service is degrading the wilderness of all the lands under its jurisdiction.

One goal of the zoning concept is, of course, to increase wildland recreational opportunities outside the wilderness cores and thus preserve the integrity of the interiors. At the same time, restrictions on some recreational uses are now, or soon will be, needed in all zones of wilderness, especially the "super-wild" cores. Fire-building, camping, and horse riding must be banned or limited where they damage the terrain intolerably. Indeed, ultimately even foot traffic necessarily will be curtailed: the ecological "carrying capacity" of specific areas must be determined and the number of visitors at any time, and during any year, kept within that capacity by requiring travel permits. The need for this is an unfortunate result of too many people and too little wilderness.

Two other purifications of wilderness are in order: the absolute freedom of the skies, which allows any pilot to over-fly wilderness as often and as close to the ground as he wishes, must be revoked; guns must be banned from wilderness areas except in legal hunting seasons.

VIII. ZERO POPULATION GROWTH IS THE ONLY HOPE OF PRESERVING WILDERNESS ON A LONG TERM BASIS.

When the wilderness movement began, America was a relatively empty land; then, our demographers predicted the nation would end up with a population no greater than 150 million people. The demographers were wrong. The larger our population grows, the harder it will become to preserve wilderness areas. Unless the populations of America and the world can be stabilized, there can be no hope for the maintenance of significant wilderness areas in the future.

Chapter 8

Small Towns

by Clayton Denman

A generation ago it was usual for urban sophisticates to look down on small town residents as "hicks" or "hayseeds." Those who had come from small-town backgrounds before establishing themselves in the big city would often try to obscure their origins.

But things have changed. Overcrowding, pollution, traffic jams, and rising prices have made cities more and more unlivable in recent years. One result has been a middle-class exodus to the suburbs, but this has frequently meant fleeing the ills of the inner city only to replace them with sterile, monotonous subdivisions. Young people particularly are coming to reject both urban and suburban patterns of living.

Small towns, once the heart of America, could represent a stimulating alternative. They are still relatively free of the social and environmental problems that plague the citics. Life in small towns has a "personal" quality lacking in anonymous urban existence. The pace is slower. Significantly, urban planners are now trying to design facilities to make possible lifestyles reminiscent of those in small towns, by building in such a way as to create closely knit neighborhoods.

At the same time, small towns are in trouble, because of lack of economic base and corporate irresponsibility. Their revival will require arresting their economic decline and, equally important, avoiding the environmental horrors which often accompany "growth."

It is important to recognize that small towns differ widely across America, which makes it crucial that they deal with their own problems. This makes it difficult to offer specific legislation, but these general suggestions for community and regional action are a beginning.

1. Small towns are often committed to the idea of "growth" and "industrial development." This is based on the misconception that the ideal is to become a city and that small towns are lagging behind such centers of advanced living as New York and Chicago. Instead, it should be recognized that smallness has its own advantages which inevitably disappear with "growth"—friendliness, quiet, compactness and diversity. Many a formerly pleasant little town has degenerated with expansion, its central section of solid old wooden houses and tree-shaded streets having become surrounded by miles and miles of hamburger stands, used car lots, shopping centers, and tract homes— all along sign-lined strips.

Development is not necessarily bad, but it should come, if possible, from within the community itself. Local development would at least make it more likely that those involved would retain some feeling for small town life and traditions. If there seems to be no choice except to encourage outside interests to enter the town, try to find small companies whose owners and managers would share the small town experience by living there.

2. All effort should be made to keep small towns from becoming "company towns." Many a mining and lumber town has been ruined by one controlling industry. Adequate zoning and sanitation provisions will help, but the main problem is to maintain some economic independence. I once studied a community of 10,000 whose city council considered an air pollution ordinance until it was informed by the only major local polluter, which employed 40 town citizens, that the plant would close if the ordinance were passed. Federal legislation should obligate industry to the small towns in which they are situated, rather than vice-versa. One approach would be to forbid government subsidies to, or purchases from, corporations that use this blackmail tactic.

3. Some small towns have matured into prosperous and sound communities by following an effective "community plan." The danger is that such workable plans encourage outsiders to settle in these towns. They are often from big cities, and want to avoid big city problems, but still have urban values and consumer expectations.

Community plans should be codified in such a way as to preserve small town values. Otherwise urban people may inadvertently destroy the places they moved to in an effort to escape the annoyances and problems of city living.

4. Growing small towns invariably need to modernize such community services as garbage disposal, sewage treatment, and water purification. Poor and elderly citizens in these towns should be protected by law from having to pay the costs of such growth. Their share of costs could be filed as no-interest liens, payable by heirs or the future purchaser of their property. Federal legislation should make funds available to keep poor or elderly citizens' housing in livable condition for the remainder of the life of the owners. The rationale behind such legislation is that it is cheaper to make repairs in the present, while deferring their payment, than to wait for inflation and further disintegration to make repairs all the more expensive. Building new housing threatens established life styles of residents and adds to the expense and difficulty of readjustment.

5. Many small towns are gradually being made over with shiny facades. But old buildings with character should be considered part of a town's natural resources and protected as such. There should be preservation codes, such as those found in Europe and some New England towns, to prevent destruction of structures of historical or esthetic interest. Zoning codes should discourage land-devouring shopping centers and instead seek to restore downtown usefulness. Shopping centers on the outskirts of small towns are usually initiated by outside investors and contribute to the demise

of independent merchants. Towns should plan their future according to the principle that outside development will do more harm than good over the long run. While money pouring into small towns may invigorate their economies, the result over a period of years is likely to be damaging to the quality of life.

Residents of small towns should also be wary of outside "planning." They must work independently on a community or regional level, and the participation of individual citizens is crucial. Here is an *outline for citizen action:*

A. Know your own town. Towns differ in significant ways.
B. Know the disadvantages, and use the advantages, of the "personal" quality of small town life.
C. Know your town's specific environmental regulations.
D. Prepare well–documented programs for solving the town's environmental ills.
E. Form an environmental coalition group.
F. Communicate your concern to others in the community.
   1. Start a newsletter or hold weekly meetings where members exchange information on environmental threats.
   2. Prepare a roster of speakers to speak in an intelligent, interesting and relatively unbiased fashion about environmental problems.
   3. Maintain good relations with the local newspaper.
   4. You will eventually have to make friends among those with economic stakes. En-

vironmental damage that is profitable to one person will always lessen someone else's business or investment opportunities.
5. Press candidates for office to declare themselves on specific local ecological issues.
6. Use students in local schools as fact-finders, work forces, and community canvassers.
7. A well-informed citizen can convince local schools to introduce ecological programs into social science and biology curricula.
8. Appoint an environmental ombudsman whom concerned citizens can call to report environmental threats or areas of inaction; and who will, in turn, be sure that action is taken.
9. Use the comparative approach to let people know how their town stacks up against other nearby communities that are building sound ecological programs. Use your newsletter to spread the word. Traditional rivalries and competition among towns can stimulate your community to action.

SMALL TOWN BIBLIOGRAPHY

Brownell, Baker, *The Human Community*. New York, Harper and Bros., 1950 (O.P.)
Brownell, who was professor of philosophy at Northwestern University, applies classical philosophy to life in small towns and bases it solidly on ecological principles.

Dean, Lois, *Five Towns: A Comparative Community Study*. New York, Random House, 1967, $2.25

Gallaher, Art, Jr., *Plainville Fifteen Years Later*. New York, Columbia University Press, 1961, $7.50

Lynd, Robert S. and Helen Merrell Lynd, *Middletown: A Study in American Culture*. New York, Harcourt, Brace and World, 1959, $2.25

————*Middletown in Transition: A Study in Cultural Conflicts*. New York, Harcourt, Brace and World, 1963, $2.45

Peterson, Elmer T., *Cities are Abnormal*. Norman, Oklahoma, University of Oklahoma Press, 1946, $3.00

Poston, Richard Waverly, *Small Town Renaissance*. New York, Harper and Bros., 1950 (O.P.)
With Brownell's book, these volumes present a detailed account of towns in Montana that tried to develop more responsive political systems within their communities.

Smith, Page, *As a City Upon a Hill: The Town in American History*. New York, Alfred A. Knopf, 1968, $6.95

Vidich, Arthur J. and Joseph Bensman, *Small Town in Mass Society*. Princeton University Press, 1968 (Rev.) $10.00, paper $2.95
This study is a thorough analysis of the influence of outside forces on the community's way of life.

West, James, *Plainville, U.S.A.* New York, Columbia University Press (1945), 1966, $1.95

Wildavsky, Aaron, *Leadership in a Small Town*. Totowa, N.J., The Bedminster Press, 1964, $7.50
Especially read Chapter 23, "A Strategy for Political Participation."

ABOUT THE SMALL TOWNS INSTITUTE

STI is a non-profit, tax deductible institution which is focusing educational resources on the problems of small towns and rural communities.

Founded in 1969, it is the only national organization developing programs exclusively for small communities. These include lectures, conferences, and workshops; curriculum and library resources development; a fellowship program; and research on technical, economic, and social problems.

These programs will help to involve local residents in a revitalization of the sense of community that could make small towns ideal places to live.

If you are interested in offering your support and membership, contact:

SMALL TOWNS INSTITUTE, P.O. BOX 517, ELLENSBURG, WASHINGTON 98926

Annual membership dues:
Individuals	$10.00
Students	5.00
Non-profit Institutions	25.00

Chapter 9

Toward a Stable Population

by Brenn Stilley

"Make Love, Not Babies."
—Bumper sticker seen in California, 1970

Just about everyone would agree that the world could use more love, but there are still many who do not realize the desperate necessity for fewer babies until the population growth rate is reduced to zero.

This is understandably often difficult to accept. Parenthood, despite its trials, seems to be instinctively gratifying, especially to women. Babies can usually warm the hardest heart, and it is truly awe-inspiring to realize that each tiny, newly-minted human being may grow up to be another Leonardo da Vinci, Shakespeare, or Einstein. (Of course, it may also grow up to be an idiot or a lunatic, however much the proud parents discount that possibility.)

As long as the world population continues to increase at its present rate, however, the

---

Author's note: This article is based on information supplied by Zero Population Growth, 330 Second Street, Los Altos, California, 94022.

TOWARD A STABLE POPULATION

baby born into it faces increasingly one of two bleak futures.

If it is born in one of the "underdeveloped countries," it is likely to grow up lacking proper nutrition, medical care, housing, and economic and political rights; among other reasons, because it is impossible for the nation into which it is born to increase production of even basic necessities at a pace which keeps up with population growth.

If, on the other hand, its life begins in one of the technological, industrial, "developed" countries, it can be expected to aggravate already existing problems such as urban overcrowding and, perhaps more importantly, diminishing of irreplaceable natural resources. As Robert and Leona Rienow describe the situation in *Moment in the Sun* (The Dial Press, 1967):

> "Every 8 seconds a new American is born. He is a disarming little thing, but he begins to scream loudly in a voice that can be heard for seventy years. He is screaming for 56,000,000 gallons of water, 21,000 gallons of gasoline, 10,150 pounds of meat, 28,000 pounds of milk and cream, 9,000 pounds of wheat, and great storehouses of all other foods, drinks, and tobaccos. These are his lifetime demands of his country and its economy."

There is no need to outline the population problem in detail here. It is brilliantly studied in all its complexity by Paul R. Ehrlich and Anne H. Ehrlich in *Population, Resources, En-*

vironment.* But two points should be discussed. It is sometimes said that the real problem is not overpopulation, but unequal distribution of resources—between "have" and "have–not" nations, and between small ruling cliques and large numbers of poor people within countries. The real priority—so the argument runs—is to equalize the distribution of wealth, with population control, if any, to follow later.

Up to a point, the argument is right. Unequal distribution of wealth *is* a tremendous problem, and effective redistribution is of paramount importance. It doesn't follow, however, that the population issue is a "red herring." To begin with, proponents of the redistribution-first theory ignore the fact that overpopulation stifles human values other than the purely material. People are not simply consumption machines. They have spiritual and esthetic needs as well, and can be starved for open space, for privacy, for freedom from herd life, as well as for food.

Even if the world's material resources could somehow be evenly divided among the planet's inhabitants overnight, the benefits would be transient. Population growth would swallow up the gains that had been made, eventually leaving those who had benefited no better off than before.

Equally important is the fact that energy requirements, pollution, and demands on non-

---

Population, Resources, Environment: Issues In Human Ecology, W.H. Freeman Co., 1970.

renewable resources vary directly with population size. There is simply no way around it. The more people there are, the less resources there are for each person, and the less likely it becomes that the "have" nations and social classes will relinquish their grip on whatever proportion of the world's draining resources they control.

Another argument sometimes encountered is that while population growth will represent a problem at some point in the future, there is still plenty of time to deal with it, since the Earth has not yet come close to the limits of its capacity. This fails to take into account the time lag inherent in all population limitation programs. If, starting today, couples began reproducing at a rate which replaced themselves and no more, the population would still continue to rise for another 80 years or so. This is because previous population growth has resulted in a proportionately larger number of younger people, whose reproductive rate is high and whose death rate is low.

The time lag principle explains why population control must begin now. When the Earth reaches the end of its capacity to support people, it will be too late to begin.

We can now turn to the federal legislative programs which are needed to help eliminate population growth in the United States. (As many have pointed out, the United States can hardly presume to speak to the rest of the world on the subject of population as long as it hasn't solved its own population problem.)

There are two main elements in these proposals. First, contraceptive information and devices, and abortions, should be made available to anyone who wants them—regardless of whether the recipient can pay for them. Second, incentives should be put into law to encourage people to limit their own procreation.

These aims will be discussed in terms of legislation which is pending as this is written. However, the reader should bear in mind that any of the bills mentioned here may be crippled by amendments, and should make sure they still include all the significant provisions before giving them his unqualified support.

Family Planning. The Population and Family Planning Act (S. 2108) was proposed by Senator Joseph Tydings (D–Maryland) on May 8, 1969. It passed the Senate on July 14, 1970, and is now under consideration by the House Committee on Interstate and Foreign Commerce.

The bill would authorize, for the first time in America's history, adequate federal funds for family planning services, population research and development, and distribution of population growth information. It authorizes funding which rises from $90 million in fiscal year 1971 to $308 million in fiscal year 1975, a total of $991.2 million over a five-year period.

Its purpose is to make comprehensive voluntary family planning services available to all Americans, regardless of income, and to continue population research so that family planning facilities will be adequate to increase demands.

To carry out these functions, an Office of Population Affairs* would be established in the Department of Health, Education and Welfare, to administer all department grants for family planning, act as a clearinghouse for information on domestic and international population programs, train workers for programs, and coordinate efforts for family planning. The bill would provide funds for:

1. Research grants to develop contraceptives and to study the sociology of family planning.
2. Family planning service agencies and similar non-profit organizations.
3. Assistance to states in planning, establishing, maintaining, and consolidating family planning services.
4. Development and distribution of family planning and population growth information, including educational materials.
5. Training grants.
6. Construction of research facilities.

Abortion. Senator Robert Packwood's (R–Oregon) District of Columbia Abortion Bill (S. 3501) removes all restrictions on abortions performed in the nation's capital, which is under Congressional jurisdiction. There is no residency requirement, and the bill's only stipu-

---

Author's note: This seems like a curious choice of words, in view of the fact that the office would presumably be working to insure that people could have affairs *without* adding to the population.

lation is that abortions must be performed by physicians. It is being considered by the Senate District Committee, but will not be acted on until the Supreme Court has ruled on the constitutionality of abortions in the District. A House equivalent has been offered by Representative Matsunaga (D–Hawaii).

Packwood's National Abortion Act (S. 3746) is currently stuck in the Senate Labor and Public Welfare Committee, where it is itself likely to be aborted out of deference to state jurisdiction. The bill invalidates existing restrictive state abortion laws and authorizes abortions for any woman who wants one, so long as it is performed by a physician.

Since there is some doubt as to federal jurisdiction over abortions, it is important to work for legalized abortions on a state level. New York, Hawaii, and Alaska have recently passed abortion legislation containing provisions similar to those in Packwood's bills. Individual citizen effort can be particularly effective in extending these reforms to other states.

Tax Incentive. Senator Packwood and Representative Paul N. McCloskey (R–California) have sponsored a measure to limit to two the number of children a taxpayer can count as tax exemptions. The bill is gathering cobwebs in the Senate Finance Committee and House Ways and Means Committee. (This particular bill has several technical flaws still to be ironed out. Most notably, it encourages having *two* children by authorizing high exemptions for the first two. Middle income families would be penalized proportionately more severely for exceeding two children than families with higher incomes.)

It should be noted that tax incentive bills like this one are designed to discourage future births, and apply only to children conceived after the passage of the bill. Nor will they work a hardship on lower income families, since they do not apply to families with an income of less than $5,500 per year.

Couples filing joint tax returns currently enjoy a financial saving as a result. Equalizing the tax rate for single people would eliminate one stimulus to marriage and procreation.

Other areas in which Congressional action on population has been proposed:

Education. Senator Tydings (D–Maryland) and Representative John Tunney (D–California) have introduced the Population Education Act. The bill would provide money to colleges and private agencies to develop public education programs and school curricula on population. It currently awaits a hearing in the Senate Health subcommittee of the Labor and Public Welfare Committee and in the House Education and Labor Committee.

Women's Rights. The birth rate in America is unlikely to be substantially lowered until women can find fulfilling roles outside of family and motherhood. Equal women's rights are supposedly covered by the Fifth and Fourteenth Amendments, but the amendments have generally proved useless to women seeking judical relief from sex discrimination. An Equal Rights amendment to the Constitution, sponsored by Senator Eugene McCarthy (D–Minnesota) and Representative William Cramer (R–Florida), is designed to remove all doubt as to the legal equality of women. Approved by the Senate Judiciary Committee, it is expected to pass the Senate. Its chances in the House Judiciary Committee, however, look doubtful.

This amendment has a long history. It has been introduced each year for the last 47, only to die in committee. The amendment has 245 co-sponsors in the House, but many of them put their names on the amendment with the expectation that it would, as usual, get stuck in committee. Such is the time-honored practice whereby representatives convince their constituents they are upholding a good cause, without ever encountering the embarrassing necessity to vote on it. A discharge petition, requiring 218 signatures, has been filed in the House to bring the bill out of committee directly to the floor.

The situation, as we go to press, is that the discharge petition has received the necessary signatures and the House voted on and passed the amendment 350 to 15.

Sex Education. Public attitudes have come a long way since the 19th century, when even the legs of a chair were delicately referred to as "limbs." Even so, sex education programs in schools are still taboo in many areas, or subject to hysterical opposition. Sex education has an important role to play in getting people used to the idea that human reproduction has social consequences and needs public debate. Politicians must sometimes be helped to locate their backbones when they appear about to yield to anti-sex education fanatics.

Local Development. The whole "growth and development" mentality needs to be opposed. Rezoning for greater density, new freeways, sewer construction for new developments, programs to attract industry, and high rise office buildings, all accommodate and encourage overpopulation. The link between rising population and declining quality of life must be repeated over and over again, if need be, until even the most backward politicians begin to understand.

Chapter 10

Eco-Pornography Revisited

by Thomas Turner

At the end of *The Environmental Handbook's* chapter on "Eco–Pornography," or environmental advertising, readers were invited to send in their own choice examples of the *genre*, for a future edition of the *Handbook*. The response was huge, and I am tempted to review in detail the ads people sent in.

I do believe that the top contender in the Eco–Pornography Sweepstakes of 1970 should not pass entirely unnoticed, even if it fails to get the recognition it so richly deserves. The pace–setter in the field is the International Paper Company, with its "Story of the Disposable Environment." This ad lovingly describes all the throw–away products they manufacture for your baby, including "Flushabye" diapers, disposable sheets, pillow cases, blankets, and even disposable furniture. It ends with a line which should become a classic: *"The disposable environment—the kind of fresh thinking we bring to every problem."*

The situation is not simply grounds for humor. Eco–pornography plays a key role in accelerating the deterioration of the American environment, not only by promoting products which add to ecological disequilibrium, but by warping people's values.

The notion of controlling advertising, through legislative or administrative regulation, inevitably brings accusations of attempted subversion of the free enterprise system. If this be subversion, make the most of it. The following preliminary suggestions are offered to legislators and their constituents. Readers should work to bring them about, as well as put their minds to work on more and better solutions to the problem.

OUTLAW ADVERTISING BY PUBLIC UTILITIES

All advertising by utilities, both publicly and privately owned, should be forbidden.

It is clear by now that all forms of energy production are harmful to the environment, in one way or another. Hydroelectric power requires damming of streams, which ruins them. Fossil fuel–burning plants contribute to air pollution, and deplete our limited resources of coal, oil, and natural gas. Nuclear plants produce byproducts such as plutonium whose disposal is difficult and dangerous, and thermal pollution. The possibility of cataclysmic accidents is thrown in for good measure. As Garrett De Bell wrote in *The Environmental Handbook,* "all power pollutes."

The only ecologically sound answer is to *cut down* on power consumption. Yet the bulk of utility companies' advertising is designed to *increase* consumption of natural gas and electricity ("Got a hang-up? Get a dryer").

For this reason, the Board of Directors of the Sierra Club recently recommended, "... immediate enactment of legislation by each of the United States to prohibit any franchised electric or gas utility, either publicly or privately owned, from engaging in any form of advertising conceived, designed or intended to cause any increase in the consumption of electricity or gas, and to prohibit any and all other activity, on the part of such utilities, to promote use of gas or electricity."

Other utility company ads pat themselves on the back for the amount of money they are spending on research to protect the environment. But it might be noted that in 1969 the power industry spent more than eight times as much money on advertising as it did on research. The advertising budget, of course, is paid for by consumers as part of their gas and electric bills. So the utilities' advertising cons people into increasing their power consumption, the companies must expand their facilities to meet the increased demand, pollution increases, profits increase, the money is spent on more plants and more advertising, which causes people to consume more power, which requires an expansion of facilities—*et cetera ad infinitum.* The process is similar to barbershop mirrors reflecting each other into the distance, forever.

There is, finally, the old argument that industries only serve the people, giving them what they want. But demand is pretty easily generated (see McLuhan or Packard) and will not be reduced as long as people are constantly told that power is always beneficent.

BEAT THEM AT THEIR OWN CON GAME

Advertising is a powerful tool and as the founder of the Salvation Army remarked, "why should the Devil have all the good tunes?" Why not advertise *back* at the eco–pornographers?

There are several instances of effective counter– or eco–advertising. The Sierra Club ads on the Grand Canyon ("Should we flood the Sistine Chapel so tourists can get a better look at the ceiling?") are credited with playing a major part in the successful effort to keep the Bureau of Reclamation from building dams in that awesome canyon. Another Sierra Club ad, "Earth National Park," helped turn on a whole generation of young people to the environmental crisis.

Perhaps the most dramatic example of all occurred in the fall of 1969, when the San Francisco Board of Supervisors decided to sell Alcatraz Island, site of the abandoned federal prison, to Texas oil millionaire H. L. Hunt. Hunt's plan would have turned the superb setting, in the middle of the San Francisco Bay, into a space museum and tourist center. Opposition failed to crystallize until San Francisco dress manufacturer Alvin Duskin put up $5,000 for a full page newspaper ad, written by advertising writer Jerry Mander (author of the Sierra Club ads), exposing the Hunt plan for the tasteless boondoggle it was. Over 8,000 pieces of mail pouring in to the Mayor and Supervisors sank the plan without a trace.

Duskin later ran an ad on the California Water Plan which elicited nearly 25,000 responses, helping along a wave of sentiment which may yet succeed in stopping the disastrous project.

Obviously, advertising like that can and does work. But it is also expensive, and where is the money to come from?

ESTABLISH A PUBLIC SERVICE ADVERTISING FOUNDATION

In the year since Friends of the Earth was formed, we have been approached by nearly a hundred advertising men, often in influential, high-paying positions, who would be willing to work on behalf of environment at a half or even a third of their present salaries. These are talented people who, like James Webb Young, "don't give a damn whether someone else sold more Quaker Oats than I sold Cream of Wheat."

To put these people to work for the environment, a Public Service Advertising Bureau should be set up. Their work to promote conservation, reduced energy consumption, smaller families, and other ecological boons could rival the most skilled products of the Madison Avenue hucksters, and reach tremendous numbers of people.

The Foundation could be managed by a coalition of national conservation groups, and would work not only on specific issues, but in educating the public to the basic—rather than cosmetic—solutions to the environmental crisis.

If private contributions or foundation grants were not enough to maintain the Foundation, other possibilities might include: a 10% tax to be levied on all advertising, or a 10% surcharge levied on clients by hip advertising agencies to fund eco–ads.

TRUTH IN ADVERTISING

Recently Congress enacted legislation requiring businesses involved in lending money or issuing charge accounts to "tell all." They now have to spell out the fact that the innocuous little provision that "bills not paid within a month will be charged at the rate of 1½% per month" means that you will be paying 18% interest per year. Things like that.

The principle should be extended to advertising. The ground rules will be tricky to decide on, but even imperfect standards are better than none. Under the new rules, Standard Oil's F–310 campaign might have to include in its ad copy the information that while F–310 is one step in the direction of reducing air pollution, it is only a microscopic dent in the problem, and doesn't come to grips with the basic issue of replacing the internal combustion engine.

Can you picture it? Gas stations would have warnings on their pumps: "Warning—Automobile emissions may be hazardous to your health." Similar warnings would be included with pesticides, herbicides, food additives, and other products threatening human or environmental health.

Legislation should require the manufacturer or advertiser to disclose, in detail, to anyone who requests the information, the process used in making his product. In other words, what did it cost the Earth to produce it? What materials are used in its production and at what cost to the environment? How many rivers were dammed to provide the electricity to run the factory?

Advertising truth standards could be implemented by a Council on Advertising Standards, with sufficient power to be effective. Its mandate should include the protection of the public interest, defined along the lines of the "Environmental Bill of Rights," drafted by Dr. Roderick Nash of the University of California at Santa Barbara. The bill declares the right of all people to have access to clean air and water, wild areas and open spaces, and food and shelter. The Council would act on citizen complaints against advertising which aggravates or covers up serious environmental problems.

THE FAIRNESS DOCTRINE

Some months ago Friends of the Earth filed a complaint against WNBC-TV with the Federal Communications Commission charging that heavy automobile and gasoline advertising constitutes a one-sided discussion of a controversial issue and therefore violates the FCC's own Fairness Doctrine.

The FCC did not agree with FOE that the earlier cigarette decision (which gave antismoking groups free TV time to run anti-cigarette spots) should be extended to cover auto and gasoline advertising, and rejected the complaint. The matter is on appeal in federal court.

However, in the adverse FCC ruling an environmental victory was achieved. The FCC said that stations must inform the public "to a substantial extent" on important environmental issues—especially including those of greatest local significance—and during prime time. If you don't think your local TV stations are living up to their environmental obligations, ask FOE (30 E. 42nd St., New York, N. Y. 10017) for information on how to get this ruling enforced in your community.

AWARDS

The movie industry has its Oscars, television has its Emmys, Broadway its Tonys, and the advertising industry its own awards presented by magazines and professional groups like the American Institute of Graphic Arts.

Occasionally the palm goes to an environmental or public service ad, but all too often the criteria for determining the winners completely ignore environmental considerations. The most recent advertising awards given by the Saturday Review—the most prestigious and coveted awards in the business—included 16 awards to power, oil, chemical, and mining companies, totaling 40% of the awards! Only three prizes were given to "do-good" organizations, and those to the highly uncontroversial American Institute of Architects, Blue Shield, and the Advertising Council itself.

A coalition of national environmental groups should establish its own advertising awards, which might fall into two categories. One group of awards would go to ads with ecological integrity, as well as graphic and literary quality, advertising ecologically sound products. Counterpart "awards" could be made for the 10 or 20 most ecologically obscene ads.

PRESSURE THE MEDIA

Newspapers, magazines, TV and radio stations, like bars, "retain the right to refuse service to anyone." They do it, too, rejecting advertising which they consider in bad taste, inappropriate to their image, or politically ticklish. Public pressure can extend their list of no-no's to include eco-pornography.

Resistance will be great. I recently wrote to *Life* to complain about a particularly offensive series of ads on Suzuki motorcycles they had been running. *Life* replied huffily that "... products that are manufactured under the law have a right to be advertised ..." and "We also feel sure that the companies you mention are also aware of their responsibility to conduct their operations at a minimum risk to the environment and are continually seeking ways to do so." Suzuki Motorcycles offered people the opportunity to ride their noisy, smoke-belching little monsters into the wilderness. Is that "minimum risk to the environment"?

If publishing and radio and TV executives are bombarded with enough complaints, they will soon at least begin dropping a few hints to manufacturers and advertising agencies.

BILLBOARDS

All outdoor advertising billboards should be banned by law. Their structures should be dismantled and recycled.

KILL THEM WITH KINDNESS

Hard as it is to believe, *Life* was probably right; companies that sponsor the most revolting ads sincerely believe that they are taking all necessary steps to respect the environment. While ignorance of biological law may be no excuse, media executives might be forgiven for reacting badly if all they hear are accusations of being evil, malicious sons of bitches. Letters of protest with an overtone of friendliness ("we know you don't mean any harm, but ...") are more likely to get results than fire-breathing invective. Most magazine editors feel they have some public responsibility. We should help educate them in what environmental responsibility truly means.

And in Dave Brower's statement we have the final, irrefutable argument: "You won't sell anything on a dead planet."

PART II

THE CONGRESS AND FEDERAL AGENCIES AND HOW TO GET THEM TO ACT

Chapter 11

Divesting the Regulatory–Industrial Complex

by Robert C. Fellmeth

This chapter will be published in expanded form as part of a book, *With Justice For Some*, to be published by Beacon Press, in December, 1970, (ed. by Mark Green and Bruce Wasserstein©)

Early in the summer of 1968, a citizen researcher working for Ralph Nader walked into the Director of Personnel's office at the Federal Trade Commission (FTC) and asked for the agency's organizational chart. He was told that no such chart existed. Later, a chart called the "Budget Control Records" was discovered, containing the non–existent information. The Director nevertheless refused to release it, on the grounds that the document was an "internal memorandum" and hence exempt from disclosure under the Freedom of Information Act. Asking for the legal basis for this extraordinary interpretation of the Act, the citizen was told that names and positions were (of course) public information, but the *salaries* of the employees were confidential. Puzzled that the amounts of public monies paid public employees could be regarded as privileged information, the student nevertheless suggested that the salaries be simply covered in the copying process or scissored off. His request was denied by the Director of Personnel and subsequently by the Executive Director of the agency.

Only by a direct appeal to the entire Commission, with the implicit threat of adverse publicity and of a law suit under the Freedom of Information Act, were the records made available. Even then, however, the FTC sought to charge a prohibitive price of $.60 per page for duplication. Since the chart was in a 30-page report format and since the student had requested eight reports going back to 1959, the cost of a single copy of the 240 pages was $144. After two months, the agency agreed to make an office copy of the records available. Ironically, this copy contained the salaries of all the employees, the supposed basis for the original denial of the records.

As graduate students and young professionals in the Ralph Nader summer study group of 1968 and 1969, investigating the responsiveness and effectiveness of the Washington bureaucracy,[1] we were totally unprepared

---

[1] The seven students in 1968 and the 110 in 1969 were graduate students or young professionals in law, engineering and medicine. The researchers in specific teams, each led by an attorney or doctor, were under the overall direction of Ralph Nader. Each team was

DIVESTING THE REGULATORY-INDUSTRIAL COMPLEX

for receptions we received—denials of the most elementary pieces of information, constant lying about events and the existence of documents, harassment of those who were discovered talking with us out of their offices, surveillance of those we were allowed to see, and, always, enormous delays.

Yet there *are* groups which do not encounter such hostility and intransigence. These are the vested interests the agencies are meant to regulate, presently existing in an incestuous intimacy with the federal bureaucracy.

This chapter will discuss the reasons for this different treatment in its appropriate context: the preferential status accorded to American industry in the formulation of federal policy, in the enforcement of federal law, and in the control of government information flow.

I. THE EMERGING REGULATORY-INDUSTRIAL COMPLEX

A. *Building the Liaison.* The existence of permanent representatives of industry in Wash-

---

assigned a specific problem area or agency. In 1969 these agencies included: food adulteration (Food and Drug Administration), rural poverty (Department of Agriculture), water pollution (Federal Water Pollution Control Agency in the Department of the Interior), air pollution (National Air Pollution Control Agency in the Department of Health, Education and Welfare) and the Interstate Commerce Commission. Most investigations culminated in the issuance of a report, sometimes with accompanying testimony in hearings. Investigators have been labeled, in the poetry of journalism, "Nader's Raiders."

ington, a political advantage the general public does not possess, has resulted in penetration of Washington agencies by the industries they supposedly regulate. First, most important decisions are made in the middle levels of the bureaucracy. It is at this stage that policy is the most malleable, and it is at this stage that industry has both formal and informal entry. Most agencies have "advisory" groups which meet and express opinions about prospective policy decisions. All of them stay in constant informal contact with industry leaders and lobbyists. Thousands of letters of complaint from consumers alleging fraud or pollution lead agencies into secret conference with industry executives, who then help draft new rules which invariably meet only the agency's public relations needs. The consumer has the opportunity to propose amendments—but only at the public hearing stage, when policy is fairly hardened. Very few, if any, agencies have consumers or consumer representatives (e.g. Consumer's Union) on any of their advisory groups, nor do they informally contact them on any *ad hoc* basis when policy is in the formative stage. Even outside groups conducting "independent" studies for federal policy guidance are carefully selected for conformity to industry view. The "outside" study which recommended that passenger trains be discontinued, more or less at railroad will, is an example. Largely devoid of environmental considerations, the report was drawn up by an outfit which has depended largely on the railroads for its business (15 of the 17 railroads seeking passenger discontinuance had conducted business with the firm).

The second aspect of this illicit relationship is the entertaining of agency personnel by their regulated industries. Industries keep file cards on most key officials, noting birthdays of sons and daughters, anniversaries, hobbies, favorite foods, and more. Consequently, officials are subject to a constant barrage of soft–sell gifts and favors. With most of these practices, it is not the monetary value that is designed to influence the recipient; it is their cumulative impact, the impression they give that people in a particular industry care about and like that official.

The extent of this process is documented in the Nader Reports from the summer of 1969. For example, Interstate Commerce Commissioners have taken approximately 220 trips during the past three years. One Commissioner has publicly estimated that twenty-five percent of the expenses are borne by industry, with the rest being borne by government. Commissioners have been regularly flying off to conferences in such meccas as Hawaii, Puerto Rico and the Bahamas to meet with industry executives—who are already well represented in Washington. The chance to visit the home state at government expense because of industry invitation is another example.

The third aspect of the regulatory-industrial liaison is job interchange. Many agencies and departments are substantially comprised of former employees of industries regulated. Conversely, attorneys view agency employment as little more than an opportunity to learn trade for later industry practice. In fact, high officials who are otherwise unqualified for executive positions with industry are offered such employment with industry while still in government. Over one-half of the former Commissioners of the Federal Communications Commission who have left in recent years are now high executives in the communications industry. Ten of twelve of the Commissioners leaving the Interstate Commerce Commission in the past decade have gone into the transportation industry directly, or have become "ICC practitioners," working for the industry. The process of the "deferred bribe" has become the normal and accepted way of maximizing the other mechanisms of influence.

The fourth aspect is the appointment and hiring process. Any potential Congressional action to control or break into the regulatory-industrial combination is negated by both pork-barrelling and campaign contributions. Industry, through a variety of devices, invests millions into the campaigns of those key Congressmen able to influence agency appropriations or appointments. The result, unsurprisingly, is the appointment to the agencies of political and corporate hacks who can be easily overwhelmed by industry domination of technical information flow. Only four of the current eleven Interstate Commerce Commissioners have had any experience with law, economics, anti-trust regulation, rate regulation, or transportation. Two of these four are from the industry regulated. All eleven had political "sponsors" and most have had a long record of party work.

The result is a convergence of regulatory and corporate views. The natural competition between specific firms is replaced by an increasingly concentrated oligopolistic structure of American industry and by hundreds of "trade associations," which lobby on behalf of combinations of firms. Since such lobbying expenses are in effect deductible (see below), and trivial compared to the millions of dollars at issue in governmental decision-making, industry spends lavishly in such efforts. Countervailing arguments from the diffuse public concerning indirect economic or environmental effects are lacking. The consumer is unorganized, unfinanced, and unrepresented. And agency personnel, even if they do not come from industry or expect to go to it, come to adopt the views which are daily put before them. The result is both a bias toward corporate rather than public interest and a favoritism in access to agency information.

B. *Preferential Treatment.* Corporations, lobbyists and trade associations do not receive the kind of reception described in the opening anecdote. In a culture where information is the currency of power, they are consistently able to get early or preferential access to documents, and reach an attentive agency audience.

In August, 1969, the existence of a Civil Aeronautics Board (CAB) report on the handling of various consumer complaints by the major airlines was discovered. The report revealed unprecedented consumer discontent with the air industry. The report was denied to the Nader group because it "mentions the names of airlines." But the information *was* released to some of the airlines and to their trade association. Thus, the supposed reason for the confidentiality, that someone might get an "undue competitive advantage," loses its credence since the airlines had the opportunity to exchange among themselves the information involved.

The National Highway Safety Bureau prereleased to General Motors an Army medical team report on off-base accidents which showed high carbon monoxide levels in auto crash victims' blood. After its secret receipt of the report, the company recalled several million cars for a "cabon monoxide hazard." Only under pressure, months later, did the National Highway Safety Bureau release the report publicly. Clearly, it should have been released to General Motors, which has an interest in the safety of its product, but why not to the public as well? They are driving the cars and they paid for the study.

Reports are frequently suppressed to protect favored corporate interests, such as the Bureau of Mines' Report on abandoned mine land collapse beneath housing developments, an ICC Report on competition in the truck industry, the report on the Task Force on Product Information outlining the government's testing results on a variety of products, a report about the growing crisis in food adulteration, another about water pollution, and even several about the bureaucracy itself by the Civil Service Commission. Yet whatever trouble we encountered relative to industry access is miniscule in comparison to that which greets a consumer writing a letter. Delay and polite evasions can easily wear down even the most zealous long-distance critics of agencies and policies.

The cost of this culture of secrecy and collusion is the diminution of democratic response mechanisms—as the public is denied detailed information about bureaucracy performance. The cost also must include misleading optimism about the crises of our time or the imminent future because of suppressed government evidence to the contrary. Finally, the cost includes the impairment of agency morale and the lack of enforcement of matters within an agency's legal mandate. The total we "pay" in these areas is undoubtedly momentous, as it involves the safety, cost, or fairness of almost everything that touches our lives.

II. THE FREEDOM OF INFORMATION ACT

The 1967 Freedom of Information Act was generally regarded as the formal guarantee of the open and public system promised by every administration. The Act required the disclosure of *all* information, at reasonable fees, to *anyone* who desired it unless the information fell within one of nine carefully defined exemptions.[2] There was no notion of "standing," that legal artifact which prevents the enforcement of many personal and civil rights on procedural grounds. This was truly to be an Act to enable the public to inquire into the nature of the government it was financing and authorizing. Further, the Act placed the burden on the government to demonstrate that a document fell within the purview of one of its exemptions.

The first ominous hint at how the Act would be enforced came when numerous Agency officials testified against the Act before Congress. As soon as the Act became law, a number of them declared that the provisions had been in effect for years and that they anticipated no need to change agency information policy because of it.[3]

Since the Act lacked provisions for punishment, and hence any deterrent effect, bureaucrats at the upper level were and are able to flout its terms with the most overweening arrogance without fear of sanction. The devices employed by federal officials to avoid compliance with the Act betray an ingenuity which could usefully be employed in the solution of problems under their jurisdiction.

A. *Denial that Information Exists.* Students investigating the Interstate Commerce Commission during the summer of 1969, as a test, requested to see information that had already

[2] Five U.S.C. ¶ Section 552 (Supp. II, 1967). For discussion of no standing aspect, see Davis, "The Information Act: A Preliminary Analysis," 34, U. Chic. L. Rev., 761 (1967).

[3] See Davis, Supra Note I, at 763.

been leaked to them. Agency officials told them with straight faces that the documents requested were not kept or were "not in the form requested."

The investigation of the Civil Aeronautics Board (CAB) yielded declarations that the following information and statistics are not kept:

1) Speeches and personal appearances made by the members of the CAB;
2) Records of the costs of investigations conducted by the CAB;
3) Travel allowances and budgetary allocations for individual Board members, the Executive Director and the Director of Community and Congressional Relations of the CAB;
4) Enforcement actions by the CAB's Bureau of Enforcement against air carriers for violations of law;
5) Complaints charging racial discrimination by the airlines;
6) The number of initial decisions of CAB hearings examiners appealed to the Board in accordance with its regulations;
7) The number of interested parties seeking to intervene in CAB proceedings pursuant to its rules of practice.

If all of this information is in fact not collected by the agency, that in itself would indicate a low level of agency performance. Of course, some of it does exist, as was later discovered by continued pressure and staff leaks.
B. *Failure to Collect Information.* Many agencies and departments collect only the kind of information that can be used by special in-

terests, not by consumers or those who might wish to judge agency performance. The ICC, for example, does not even bother to count or classify its thousands of letters of complaint from consumers. It keeps no data whatsoever on its most-used sanction, the "request for voluntary compliance."

The FTC was asked if it records the size or sales volume of violators of deceptive practice statutes. The agency's response was: "Annual sales are not maintained as general information in deceptive practice matters. This is simply because sales volume is frequently one of the many considerations in assessing the impact of a particular practice." Of course, if no information is kept, sales would seem to be not "one of the many" factors but no factor at all.

Agencies and departments "trust" the corporations they are intended to regulate to provide nearly all of the information upon which the "regulation" rests. Thus, the ICC accepts, without detailed verification, railroad estimates of increased expenses justifying massive price hikes. It relies substantially on the Association of American Railroads to supply information about car shortages. It "trusts" the industry to "volunteer" information about interlocking directorates and possible illegal dealings with subsidiaries. Special agents and investigators admit that even when they find violations— which they add are common—the agency prefers to ignore their reports rather than pursue the more difficult and pressured course of litigation. One agent said that it was as if his reports on these matters "dropped off the end of the earth." Another described some of these violations as "a loud belch in a church—a resounding noise that didn't occur."

C. *Minimal Disclosure and Distribution.* The Federal Trade Commission discloses only in a formalistic sense assurances of voluntary compliance and compliance reports, documents which concern sanctionless requests by the FTC to businessmen to cease illegal activity. The only text of such reports which the Commission permits to be made public is extremely general and conclusory. A single copy of each is placed in ring binders in the docket room of the agency's central office building in Washington, D.C. No copies are made or distributed to anyone, and no news releases on them are issued. It is an exaggeration to say that these texts are made "public."

There have been more direct tactics to limit physical access to supposedly "public" information. Two investigators discovered that some pamphlets they had been reading in a Department of Agriculture (Pesticides Regulation) library were removed over-night when officials learned of their interest in them.

Another twist to the minimal distribution game is the charging of outrageous fees for "searching for a document" and for "reproducing" it. Many agencies charge $2 search fee for each document requested and will refuse to combine documents. Thus 25 documents will cost $50, even though they are together in the same file. Then the agency may not permit removal of the document from the office—they must duplicate it. Some charge for this service is reasonable, but most agencies charge $.50 per page and more for duplication.

D. *Contamination.* Many agencies arrange their records in such a way that public information is inextricably intertwined or connected with allegedly confidential information. Separation is then ruled "impossible." The Department of Defense is a veteran deployer of this tactic. For example, they refused to reveal information of the quantity of oil being pumped from the bilges of naval ships. Their refusal was based on the grounds that this information, although not confidential in itself, was going to be included in a report which would contain some operational data that *was* classified.

Likewise, the Department of Labor has claimed that it can release nothing from its files on the Walsh-Healey Act since *part* of the file is considered confidential—even though the requested information was admittedly public and admittedly separable, and goes back to 1936, when the Act was first passed. Thus, there is no way to evaluate the administration of the law in its one-third of a century of history.

E. *Delay.* If none of the first four tactics are available, an agency will use delay to wear down and discourage those seeking information. The first device which facilitates this process is the establishment of a multi–layered appeal procedure. Most agencies require a denial by the custodian of the information, a written denial (after a written request) by the Managing Director or General Counsel (sometimes one, then the other) and finally a written request and a written denial by the Chairman or appointed head of the agency or department. Delays of several weeks between each tier are common. Yet even more common were simple delays by individual officials in response to information requests. Richard McClaren, head of the Department of Justice's Anti-Trust Division, took three months to answer (and deny) one student's request to interview four attorneys in his division.

F. *Misuse of Exemptions.* Probably the most direct and popular technique, when all of the above are inappropriate, is the broad interpretation of the exemptions of the Freedom of Information Act which specify allowable secrecy. The Act states that, among others, "investigatory files," "inter-agency or intra-agency memoranda," "internal rules or procedure," and "information given in confidence" need not be divulged. Although each of these exemptions was carefully framed to prevent its misuse, the agencies have interpreted them so broadly that they completely swallow the Act.

Anything from the field is part of an "investigatory file." Department of Labor records ten to fifteen years old on Walsh-Healey Act violations are still "under investigation for prospective prosecution." And the Federal Trade Commission, immediately after the passage of the Act, seemed to classify every noun in the language as "under investigation." Every company, every advertisement, *everything* was confidentially "under investigation." It was puzzling how few of these matters ever appeared on the agency's formal docket. Of those that did appear, sometimes from continual requests for information, they then remained there interminably.[4]

The extensive delays occurring during "investigations" permit the open-ended use of the "investigation" exemption. FTC investigations into the food industry, odometers, petroleum, analgesics, soft wood lumber, lottery game gimmicks and many others have taken from four to forty years.[5] Often, investigations end without result.

Anything originating from Washington is considered an "internal procedure" or an "inter– or intra–agency memorandum." Thus, the Department of Agriculture denies the minutes of meetings with "industry advisory groups," including the National Food Inspection Committee and the Poultry Advisory Committee. Civil Service Commission reports on the FTC

---

[4] If possible, those who wish to suppress information which is controlled by others will make personal requests to withhold. Thus, although the Freedom of Information Act does not except Congressional agency correspondence from disclosure (Congress is not considered an "agency" under the "inter-agency" exemption), four Commissioners of the ICC approached the Senate Commerce Committee and personally and privately asked that we be denied access to correspondence between them and the Committee.

[5] Of the 4.17 years it takes the FTC, on the average, to open an investigation and issue an order, over two years is spent on the "investigation." One case has been on the docket since 1947. Another case was in process for more than five years before the FTC learned that the defendant company had been dissolved, one year after the start of the investigation.

and the ICC, statistical breakdowns of complaints received from consumers, and results of government product testing are placed under this exemption. An FTC attorney, when asked the number of attorneys in his bureau—a simple enough request—stated that this was confidential (an "internal procedure").

In sum, a law which was to help guard the guardians is being adroitly avoided; the obvious reason for the "massive resistance" is that those whom the law would regulate are also those who implement the law. It is analogous to the futile practice of filing complaints against the police with the police, but it is far more serious. Information, particularly timely information, is the *sine qua non* of a functioning democracy. When citizens lack access to information channels, while organized, special interests have easy access, a corporate oligarchy, not a representative democracy, results. A wave of citizen hope has succumbed to an undertow of bureaucratic ingenuity—and fear.

III. FEAR OF EXPOSURE

A. *Upper Echelon Fear: The Image and the Reality.* Student investigators found two fundamentally different categories of fear. There was the fear of appointed officials and upper staff that we would embarrass them by disclosing information they prefer to keep confidential. Secondly, there was the fear from the lower to middle level staff, who were often eager to discuss the workings of their agencies but feared for their job security and career possibilities.

The fear of upper staff was manifest when Paul Rand Dixon, then Chairman of the Federal Trade Commission, physically forced investigator John Schulz out of his office when the latter asked about the basis for an information denial. Mr. Dixon then called his upper staff to instruct them that the "FTC investigators" were to be locked out, that no one was to communicate with us. One reason for the banishment was that we had already learned much about the agency, including the fact that the Chairman had put an agency field office in Oak Ridge, Tennessee, in the district of Rep. Joe Evins, Chairman of the House Committee responsible for overseeing the agency and its appropriations. (Philadelphia and Detroit, among other major cities, did not have offices; moreover, the Oak Ridge office was headed by Judge Geer, an old crony of Rep. Evins).

Why do these officials fear exposure of their agency's activities? It is because image is the reality of Washington. Officials and upper staff will keep their jobs only so long as they can respond to forces which threaten them. This end can usually be accomplished through private accommodations; but if there is a major threat to the favorable image of the agency through the action of an individual, officials and upper staff realize that higher authorities might be compelled to investigate publicly.

The revelation of private dealings between industry and special interests, to the detriment of the public, would do great harm to the agency's image, its lifeblood. Agencies consider it necessary to maintain a low visibility situation in order to protect this regulatory-industry collusion.

B. *Lower Echelon Fear: Weaving the Shroud.* The fear at the lower to middle level is different. It is not the fear of an embarrassing disclosure, *per se,* but of retaliation by superiors for relating something which might conflict with the official agency version. This is the fear that enabled Chairman Dixon to enforce successfully his illegal edict. Few employees of the Federal Trade Commission would in fact talk with us after the order. A young attorney at the Federal Trade Commission who had exchanged some pleasantries with a student in the hall of the FTC office building was subsequently warned by his division chief to "be careful of his conduct" because the FTC was "back on its heels under criticism." Fearing unfavorable job recommendations from the agency upon departure, he canceled a prospective interview and would not talk with us in public further.

The fear at the lower level is also manifested in a myriad of subtle ways. It is an official who refuses to be interviewed alone, but insists on having another attorney or his superior present. It is requiring that a stenographer be present to record verbatim what is said, or writing copious "memos to the files" after an interview. It is lower and middle staff refusing to reveal even the most innocuous information, afraid to express even basic opinions about their responsibilities. It can be seen in sweaty palms and nervousness during an interview.

The institutionalization of this lower staff fear is accomplished through sophisticated enforcement mechanisms.

1. *The agency line.* Most agencies and departments carefully construct an official "agency line" or stock response concerning controversial issues. Rarely do these responses have any relation to reality, but they are repeated with such uniformity within and by the agency, that mere repetition imbues them with a kind of sanctity. Thus, the Federal Trade Commission cannot investigate ghetto frauds because of the "interstate commerce clause of the Constitution." The Interstate Commerce Commission can do nothing about home-moving frauds because it "lacks jurisdiction." And the Food and Drug Administration cannot move "too fast" against the marketing of dangerous drugs. Outside the agencies these answers are derided by those familiar with the laws involved. The relevant statutory and constitutional clauses allegedly restraining the FTC and the ICC in the examples have been liberally interpreted for the past decade, but the agencies themselves have yet to utilize them. And the FDA *can* move quickly against an unsafe drug. Most of these bureaucratic positions are self-fulfilling prophecies.

The agency line is often codified in the agency's annual report. The categories now and then change, but the tone and purpose of the annual report remain constant. It is de-

DIVESTING THE REGULATORY-INDUSTRIAL COMPLEX 149

signed to project an aura of careful progress toward the solution of current problems. They are difficult problems, yes, but the department has made great strides, as the increasing numbers of enforcement actions from year to year in all categories prove. And although the problem is not quite yet solved, solution is imminent. For instance, one can go back to the initial case before the Interstate Commerce Comission, the first large regulatory agency created back in 1887, and read about a group of small farmers complaining that the railroad refused to supply them with boxcars because they claimed a shortage. One can then follow this matter from annual report to annual report, all the way to 1970. Each year one learns that the "boxcar shortage" problem, which once again forced many of America's small farmers to dump their harvest, will be solved in a very short time. There is never an indication that the ICC, in reality, has done virtually nothing in the area except protect big business, refusing to prosecute cases of massive violation of the law submitted by the agency's own special agents in the field.

Appearance is crucial. This requires that the annual report this year must be more impressive than last year's. Since accomplishing the agency's mission would, if done in an optimum way, result in the end of the agency, the only way to increase numbers year after year is to prosecute more trivial, less important violations, a mis-emphasis not reflected by annual report tables. Therefore, agency personnel in the field are directly told to meet a certain quota[6]—and told that it does not matter what kind of case it is, as long as they do *more* than was done last year.[7]

The lower to middle level employee soon learns that it is hands-off big business, hands-off innovative prosecutions to counter innovative violations of law, and hands-off offending those who might threaten political pressure—i.e., major campaign contributors to key Congressmen, industries dominated by former upper staff personnel or by the company the employee's superior just left or just received a job offer from.

2. *Structure.* Agencies are structured, though not necessarily intentionally, to aid in the enforcement of secrecy. Most are tightly compartmentalized. Departments are divided into bureaus, sections, offices and desks. A veteran

---

[6] See, for example, instructions from Washington to ICC Special Agents to this effect, we produce in Chapter 12, *Surface Transportation, the Public Interest in the ICC,* by this author, issued on March 12, 1970.

[7] It is similar to a housewife who discovers a leak in her basement. Instead of hiring a plumber, she gets three people to continually mop up the dripping. Since the chief mopper would like to expand his business, he is going to recommend more moppers and more mopping. He is not going to be anxious to repair the leak. If he could write an annual report for the public, he would probably say that "the leak is lessening and the water on the floor is gradually dissipating. We have increased our output from six bucketfulls a day to seven, and anticipate further progress." Then he might add, in order to appear aggressive, "We have requested from Congress the authority to use larger mops and will do so upon passage of this pending legislation."

DIVESTING THE REGULATORY-INDUSTRIAL COMPLEX 151

of twenty years or more in one office is likely to have no idea what is happening in the office down the hall. Rigid lines of communication permit the isolation of a given report, meeting or incident among a limited group. Those who would most likely reveal it are among the younger employees at the GS-9 to GS-12 levels, those who have less to lose by exposure of complicity with industry. But because of the compartmentalization, together with a policy of letting only a few of the younger staff participate in any one decision or matter, it is relatively easy for the entrenched upper staff to trace down leaks.

3. *Surveillance.* Complementing agency structure is a pervasive fear and anticipation of surveillance, including electronic surveillance.[8] We were struck by the reticence of many otherwise friendly agency employees to say anything significant while in their offices. But we were frequently told at lunch or at their homes that they fear an electronic bug in their offices. Most of them suspect other agencies or their superiors, and some point to the lucrative

---

[8] Robert Kennedy, while Attorney General, was discussing a serious policy matter with one of his staff, when he commented that he wanted to convey the problem to FBI Director J. Edgar Hoover. His aide said, ominously, "he already knows by now," at which point Kennedy, understanding his meaning, began shouting, "Do you hear me Edgar, do you hear me Edgar?"

Also Tom Wicker has recently reported that a major Democratic contender for the Presidency would only be interviewed *outside* his normal office because he feared that his office was bugged.

business conducted by electronic eavesdropping device manufacturers, which have large and busy offices in Washington. Agency officials feel that any criticisms about policy expressed by them may be relayed to the industries and to their contacts higher up in the agency. Since surveillance development is advanced over anti-surveillance detection and jamming, there is little these men can do to verify or alleviate their fears, even if they had the resources to do so.

Non-electronic surveillance is equally prevalent and intimidating. A high official in the Nixon administration asked two departments we were studying to submit detailed memos on our activities, including a list of all personnel interviewed. The ICC circulated a memorandum requesting staff to record how much time we spent talking with them and to summarize the contents of the conversations.[9] Other agencies went even further. Assistant Secretary of the Department of the Interior (DOI), Carl Klein, first agreed to cooperate with our study of the Federal Water Pollution Control Agency (FWPCA), which is within DOI's jurisdiction. Later, however, he refused to permit us to interview any of the public employees in the Agency or Department. Mr. Klein persisted in his lock-out until rising pressures of adverse publicity compelled him to rescind his illegal bar. However, Mr. Klein's own staff assistant, Jeffrey Stern, and the FWPCA Director of the Program Analysis, Richard Nalesnik, were specifically assigned to monitor our interviews.

---
[9] *Id.*

DIVESTING THE REGULATORY-INDUSTRIAL COMPLEX 153

They openly acknowledged their role as such on several occasions. Further, they were told to report to Mr. Klein, himself, and to his deputy, Robert L. McCormick, who also admitted the existence of the policy. Mr. Klein nevertheless brazenly denied it to the Washington *Post,* stating that "as far as I know" there were no monitors. Not only Mr. Klein's misuse of power in his "monitoring," but also his willingness to "create news"—no matter how obvious the lie might be to personnel within the agency—must impress agency employees who might be tempted to speak their minds. Of course, this kind of monitoring is rarely if ever required of the daily deluge of visitors from trade associations, corporations, and other special interest groups.

4. *Sanctions.* The critical element necessary to enforce secrecy and strict adherence to the agency line is the power of effective sanctions. The obvious sanctions are the denial of sought-after rewards, such as grade level advances. In addition, there are other sanctions, ranging from a sudden surge of undesirable assignments to the more extreme measure of dismissal. Even if matters do not progress to this point, their potential use is a sufficient deterrent to older, security-conscious bureaucrats.

5. *Natural Selection.* These sanctions are complemented by a system of natural selection. Agencies recruit and promote personnel who will be most affected by these sanctions. Those who question assumptions or who demonstrate aggressiveness or imagination are generally dis-

couraged. The turnover rate at the lower professional levels (GS-9 to 12) of most agencies is staggering, partly because only those lacking in creativity and critical capacity are made welcome. Many agencies rotate out, usually by the voluntary resignation of the discouraged or disgusted, one-third or more of the new recruits at these levels each year. Those that remain acquire an increasing interest in job security as they rise to more powerful positions. Their opportunity for new careers, especially without favorable job recommendations from the government, declines as the years pass. They become adjusted to passive acceptance of the agency line. Often, the men most acceptable to control move from complicity to a role of active suppression.

The intensity of the process can be inferred from the longevity of those who have survived the selection process to reach positions of power. At the ICC, the average tenure of the present bureau directors is 31 years. The lack of new blood infusion aids the development of cronyism, illustrated by the FTC, where until recently *every* attorney bureau director came from a small Southern town, as did Chairman Dixon who promoted them.

IV. CONCLUSION

What is essentially happening in America is the collusion of the two great forces in our society: government and industry. Separate, they are subject to some public influence over both.

The combination eliminates the primary difference between our system and that of the Soviets.

The reinvigoration of government regulatory agencies will require substantial changes in the procedures under which they now operate.

First, officials must be appointed on the basis of qualification. This seems to be a simple truism, but it will require public attention to appointments previously made to accommodate industry. Appointments must not be "cleared" with industry, as is presently the norm.

Second, job interchange, at least the "deferred bribes" of upper level appointees, must be ended. This can be done by requiring, as a condition of appointment, that anyone taking a position may not accept employment from an industry regulated by the government body involved for at least five years after leaving the government post.

Third, there must be an adversary process in agency proceedings, with someone representing the counter-corporate side. There must be independent consumer counsel, with a full staff within each agency, as well as consumer representation on all formal advisory groups. Only then can favoritism to corporate interests be corrected. Currently Congress is considering a bill to implement this proposal by setting up an independent consumer agency to represent the public interest. This bill is popularly known as the Nader Bill or Consumer Agency Bill.

Fourth, there must be tight policing of campaign contributions from industry, with limitations and disclosure requirements actively enforced. There should be a change in tax laws permitting deductions for contributions to candidates by private individuals, thus broadening the contributive base of officials. Further, free television time should be provided for candidates to minimize the importance and necessity of heavy financial aid for this purpose.

Fifth, tax laws relating to lobbying must be changed. At present, corporations are allowed to deduct their lobbying costs as business expenses. Individuals who attempt to counter the lobbying efforts of these special interests, however, are denied the same privilege. In fact, organizations formed to represent a public interest are threatened with loss of their tax deductible status if they try to influence elections and legislative acts. Just recently, the IRS withdrew tax deductible status from the Sierra Club because of its battle to save the Grand Canyon. A general warning was also issued to universities that their political activity centering around the Indochina War and the 1970 elections could result in the loss of their tax exempt-tax deductible status. This should be reversed. IRS Code Section 501(c)3 and (c)4 should be changed, so that organizations seeking to influence elections and legislation for public rather than private gain need not risk losing financial support. On the other hand, these activities, if connected directly or indirectly with enterprise based on economic gain, should *not* be deductible.

Sixth, there must be active trust-busting of both corporations and their trade associations.

Most, if not all, of America's top 500 corporations should be split into competitive entities. The largest, General Motors, could just as easily be Buick, Pontiac, Chevrolet, etc., with no loss in efficiency, but great benefit to the consumer and the public. Any industry-wide research or agreement necessary for the public interest should be accomplished by or through the government. The awesomely powerful trade associations should be dissolved by law. The result would be to minimize the corrupting organized power of the special interests.

Seventh, there should be legal redress under federal and state laws for parties as a class. This means that a suit could be brought against a corporation to seek compensation for damage resulting from faulty products. If the suit was won, compensation would be paid not only to those bringing suit, but also to all others in the aggrieved class. This is the only way general public interests can be directly heard within our judicial system. The law should leniently define representation requirements and establish a clear cause of action on a class basis for consumer grievances. Senator Tydings' class action bill currently before Congress implements this proposal.

Eighth, Congressional oversight committees must be given adequate staff to scrutinize their respective agencies and departments. Staffs are presently so small that it would require a tenfold increase to achieve the scrutiny necessary for even elementary Congressional control of the bureaucracy. Finally, the seniority system must be ended, reducing the power of committee chairmen whose position, following a corporate-financed campaign, is presently assured.

Ninth, and probably most important, the Freedom of Information Act should be amended to:

a) impose contempt sanctions for repeated violations of court orders compelling disclosure under the Act,
b) specify minimal, at-cost charges agencies may levy for the reproduction of documents requested under the Act,
c) mandate broad court orders to compel compliance with the spirit of the Act when upper level officials subvert the Act through harassment of those who legally reveal information requested under the Act,
d) specifically limit current exemptions.

Chapter 12

Reforming Congress—
First Order of Business

by Congressman Morris K. Udall and Congressman Paul N. McCloskey

The fight for a better environment—or to preserve what we have—is going to have to be fought in many arenas. The courts, government agencies, board rooms of private corporations —all of these will be involved. But perhaps some of the biggest battles ahead will have to be fought in the Congress. For those who want to get involved in this cause it would be well to have an understanding of what the Congress is, how it functions, and what changes are needed to make it truly responsive to such a general need as a decent environment for the people of this country.

What is Congress? As it has functioned in the past, it can be described as a forum in which many specialized and particular interests are balanced against each other, producing national policies which take these contending interests into account.

An example would be our labor laws. Whenever any important change is contemplated in labor policy, the forces of organized labor and organized management are brought to bear on the Congress, its committees and its members. The end product is always some kind of compromise between these opposing forces. In most cases the general public interest is well enough served, and the process can be said to work reasonably well.

But at times this process doesn't work so well. Sometimes it's not enough for the whole of national policy to be fabricated out of such individual parts, tailored as they are to benefit particular groups or interests. For example, in a battle between the railroads and railroad workers, will it always be true that a compromise between these particular interests will exactly coincide with the interest of the public at large? Or when Congress hammers out a middle position between the interests of mining and the interests of cattle-raising, can we be certain the result is invariably in line with the interests of ordinary citizens everywhere?

The danger in this system—the way Congress operates on most issues today—is that often only the intense, special interests will be adequately heard, to the exclusion of more vaguely articulated interests of the general public.

Time and again, watching legislation make its way through the Congress, one is prompted to ask, "Why isn't there a people's lobby to speak up for all the people of this country who aren't being heard on this issue?" And yet there

REFORMING CONGRESS 161

is no "people's lobby" to fill this need; the organized, dues-paying, letter-writing, campaign-contributing pressure groups of the country continue to carry weight in congressional decision-making far in excess of the actual numbers of citizens they represent. This is not to say that they are all bad; most of them serve very legitimate purposes. But they do not generally represent the interest of the public at large.

And that is why people having a concern about the environment must have a concern, too, about Congress and the way it operates. For if there is one cause that is general in nature, that involves the welfare of the entire population and not just one segment of it, that cause is the environment.

Suppose we consider the problem of air pollution—we all breathe the stuff and therefore have a vital interest in what is done about it. Let's say that what is needed is a tough crackdown on industrial smoke and extremely rigid and costly standards for the automobile industry. Proposals of this kind are made and referred to committees. What happens now? Automobile manufacturers, employing the best lawyers, scientists and expert witnesses, argue that such standards would be unrealistic and harmful to the economy. Equally articulate and effective spokesmen for manufacturers' groups come in with volumes of data to prove that industrial smoke is an insignificant part of the air pollution problem. Perhaps labor groups come in to argue that standards of this kind would throw men out of work, creating chaos in many industrial centers. And so on; the representatives of various special segments of our society make certain that *their people* are heard, that their special problems and needs are taken into account in the writing of new laws affecting them.

But what about you and your neighbors, who belong to none of these groups and perhaps have conflicting interests—you people who merely breathe the air the other people insist they must pollute? It's sad, but a fact, that your interests are not likely to be presented by anyone in particular. And whoever does speak for the cause of clean air will do so without any special authority or mandate to represent you or the public as a whole; in fact, he will probably be seen as a spokesman for just one "protectionist" group or another without any real weight in public affairs.

This is not to say that Members of Congress are oblivious to the general interest we all have in clean air, clean rivers and lakes. Many congressmen are keenly interested, and they are aware of the need before a single witness is heard or letter received. But as Congress operates in a political system—always conscious of reactions in the home district, always concerned about the next election—it naturally occurs that the more effective and better-articulated views of *some* citizens will carry more weight than any vague claim that might be made concerning the so-called public interest.

Since politics is seen as the "art of the possible," congressmen know they're not going to create the millennium overnight, or with a single bill. They know just so much progress is possible at any given time; they know that the range of options open to them is limited by the current state of public opinion, the current makeup of the Congress, the policies of the current administration, etc. And, therefore, they may vote for a watered down and quite inadequate bill on air pollution, not because they think it's the best bill they could write but because they think it's the best bill they can pass.

In most cases, the distinction between the "perfect" and the "possible" is a subjective one that has been influenced to a great degree by the manner in which Congress is organized and carries on its work.

In our view, Congress will continue to see its options restricted, its innovative role limited, until changes are made in its method of operation. These changes fall into three categories:

1. To make it impossible for measures of genuine public support to be bottled up in committee.
2. To induce congressmen to take a broader viewpoint by forcing their votes and legislative actions to be made a matter of public record.
3. To enable Congress to function more effectively and in a more democratic fashion, thereby making it more responsive to a cross-section of pressures within our political system rather than to just certain of these pressures having particular access to the system as it is now organized.

The reader whose concern is protecting his environment may find some of these reforms unduly parochial or technical in nature. Yet it is just such technical barriers which can prevent an environmental bill from coming to a vote or being enacted into law.

THE SENIORITY SYSTEM

The seniority system under which both houses of Congress operate is a major and perhaps the primary target of most advocates of congressional reform. Although this system is viewed by many as a hallowed tradition, it goes back no further than 1910 in the House and 1915 in the Senate. It is unique to the American Congress, without parallel in any state legislature or any foreign parliament in other countries. Under the seniority system, the member of the majority with the longest continuous service on a committee automatically becomes the chairman of that committee. Since the chairman's powers are usually substantial, the seniority system can be seen to play a very important part in influencing the decision-making process of Congress. Usually it is the chairman who decides which bills will be considered and when, who sets the style and pace of the committee. If a bill is to be ignored or killed, it is usually the chairman who makes that decision.

Yet the seniority system isn't all bad. It has the virtue of eliminating internal politics and jockeying for position. It guarantees that the congressmen chosen to head committees be men of experience in the work of those committees. And finally, the system prevents the kind of centralization of power which might result if chairmanships were determined by the party leadership in some way.

Opponents of the seniority system argue that it violates the primary safeguard of democracy —the ability of the people to change the course of events through the election process. Since the committee chairman is elected by only a small portion of the national electorate, and is usually from a safe district (without which he probably would not have survived long enough to become chairman), nothing forces him to be responsive to the concerns of other parts of the country, or to broad national needs.

Opponents argue that this basic weakness contributes to many related problems. Power, they say, has been fragmented far beyond what was intended. The result is that Congress is divided up into a myriad of virtually autonomous suzerainties, each with tight control over a certain area of national legislation.

It is true that committee members are usually reluctant to challenge their chairman on major or even minor issues, and in most cases it is exceedingly difficult for the members of the committee to override the views of their chairman short of a disruptive, all-out revolt. Furthermore, the power of the committee chairman to decide which bills struggle forward and which die in a desk drawer means that one man from one district or one state can be in a position to block action favored by a majority of the members of the whole House or Senate. There are certain procedures, such as the discharge petition in the House, which theoretically provide the membership with the means of overruling an obstinate committee, but in practice these procedures have not proved effective. Congress may be the heart of our democratic system, but it bypasses democratic procedures in many of its most important decisions.

Opponents also argue that the current system provides no alternative to strict seniority. There is no way to relieve an ineffective or arbitrary chairman of his duties, and all factors other than length of service—such as leadership qualities, intelligence, ability, and consonance of his views with those of a majority of his own party—are ignored in the selection process. The result, it is argued, is to make Congress an isolated, ingrown institution essentially unresponsive to the real needs of the country.

What, then, should be done? Many specific proposals have been advanced, varying considerably in the extent to which they would depart from the present system. Seniority was one of the topics assigned to a special commission of the Democratic Caucus of the House in the spring of 1970. Similar interest in revision of the seniority system has been shown by the Republican Caucus this past year. Whatever the precise proposals turn out to be, we feel their thrust should clearly be to make the committee system more responsive both to the membership of the Congress and to the country as a whole. If proposals of this kind can be placed into effect, the result will be a much greater awareness of the general public interest and a much greater responsiveness to demands of the public at large, rather than special segments of it. The environment cause would certainly be one of the greatest beneficiaries.

Proposals for reform of the seniority system have one thing in common—they would all limit somewhat the authority of the committee chairman. In almost every other respect they differ. Following are the major proposals which have been made:

- Election of the chairman by a secret ballot of the majority members of the committee.
- Election of the chairman by all members of the majority caucus.
- Nomination of the chairman by the party leadership with the approval of a majority of the party caucus.
- A requirement that no single geographic section of the country have more than 50% of the chairmanships of the major committees.
- Rotation of the chairmanship between the two most senior committee members of the majority party.
- Limiting a chairman's term to a fixed period of time.
- Requiring the chairman to relinquish his post upon reaching a certain age.
- Making a member who opposes his party's platform in that committee's area of responsibility ineligible for election as chairman.
- Requiring the appointment of a vice chairman so that the committee can function when the chairman is absent.

Making it possible for the members of a committee to remove the chairman on a vote of a certain percentage of the membership.

Even among the proposals for election of chairmen by secret ballot of the party caucus there are many differences. It has been suggested that any member of the committee should be eligible, that the chairman should be elected from among the three most senior members of the committee (or from the three most senior after the current chairman has reached age 70), that the senior member of the committee should be voted up or down by the caucus, and if defeated, the next most senior would stand for election in the same manner; that the senior member would be chairman unless another committee member were nominated and received the vote of 2/3 of the caucus; and that all members with more than a given number of years of service should be considered equal in seniority and the chairman selected from among them.

There are, of course, advantages and disadvantages to each of these proposals, which is one reason reformers have been unable to agree on a single plan. There are, however, certain guidelines which can be used in evaluating the possible effect of various reform proposals.

First, any change should, we think, result in committee chairmen and ranking minority members being more responsive to individual colleagues and to the nation as a whole—that is, more aware of their national responsibilities as distinguished from the responsibilities of their own constituencies. The attitude of committee chairmen toward junior members would change dramatically if they knew that in some way their continuation in office depended upon the votes of these junior members. They would be more likely to listen to the views of their colleagues. In turn, the public, by making its views known to the members of Congress, would have a greater influence over the chairman's decisions and therefore on the course of legislation.

Second, the possibility of reprisal by a chairman against members who opposed him in his election should be minimized by the use of a secret ballot. The same device should have the effect of reducing conflict and infighting.

Third, the ideal system would give weight to qualifications for leadership positions which do not coincide necessarily with the length of a man's service. At the same time, the system should continue to take note of the importance of experience and insights gained through extensive service.

Fourth, any change adopted should contribute to the rational functioning of our two-party system. It should make it possible for the Congress to carry out in a meaningful way the principles set forth in party platforms and accepted by the voters as the policies they want their government to pursue. No longer should it be possible for a single individual, who may be out of step with the rest of the country, to obstruct the implementing of new policies sought by the voters of this country. With this kind of change parties would have to be more responsible in adopting platforms, voters could choose a party on the basis of explicit programs, and the desires of the general electorate could be more directly transmitted into the laws of the land.

Finally, the reform should be such that it enables Congress to regain its ability to act forcefully and decisively. With power in the hands of nearly independent committees, there is a certain lack of cohesive action and direction in the work of the Congress. A shift of the power center to elected leadership would allow Congress to move and act more often as a policy initiating body, resuming a coequal role with the executive branch. This would enable the Congress to command greater confidence from the people of this country. At the same time, procedural change should not allow a return to near-dictatorial power by one man as Speaker. Rather, the Speaker should be able to lead the party through personal prestige and power of persuasion, but at the same time he and the majority leader and the committee chairmen should become a more unified policy group guiding the majority as the minority leader and ranking minority members would guide the other party.

One final comment may be in order. Often, the argument against the seniority system is couched in very personal terms against specific individuals. This misses the point. It may be that under any of the proposed reforms we have listed most of the present committee chairmen would continue in power. It is a fact that the seniority system, with all of its defects, has brought into power a great many truly outstanding committee chairmen. Nevertheless, by depriving chairmen of guaranteed tenure of indefinite duration, Congress would certainly guarantee that all chairmen would show greater concern and respect for the views of their colleagues and, in turn, the general public, since support would be needed for continuation in the position of chairman at some future time. Thus, a single change in the selection process might make committee chairmen, even if they should be the same men, more responsive to the national will on matters coming before their committees.

THE OPEN SYSTEM

Perhaps because of past criticism, the Congress has been giving increasing attention to various other proposals having the intent of making the Congress more responsive to the needs of the country. A number of these proposals were scheduled to be debated in connection with a congressional reorganization bill coming up in the last months of the 91st Congress.

One such change would revise the system of nonrecorded, "teller" voting which in the past has prevented the public from knowing how individual congressmen voted on particular issues. (In a teller vote, members form lines, one for each side of the question, and a clerk counts them as they pass but records no names.) Under this proposal one-fifth of a quorum (44 members) could demand that teller votes be recorded, providing a record of how each member voted. Since almost all amendments are decided in the House by standing, voice or teller votes, with no record of how individual members voted, a change of this kind could have considerable impact upon the outcome of many closely-fought issues.

This change could be of great importance. Typically, only one-third of the membership participates in teller votes, some of which decide extremely important issues. On the other hand, eighty to ninety per cent of the House is usually recorded on formal roll call votes. In the first few months of the 1970 session of Congress non-record teller votes decided such issues as the use of funds for American forces in Indochina, appropriations for the antiballistic missile, the C-5A transport, MIRV missiles and the B-1 bomber; amendments limiting the ability of the federal government to seek further school desegregation; and the budget for the space administration. An attempt to delete further funding for the SST airliner, an issue in which many environmentalists took great interest, was defeated by a margin of only 16 votes (86-102) on a non-recorded teller vote. Only 188 of 435 members, or forty-three per cent of the House membership, voted on that important question.

It is uncertain that any of these issues would have been decided differently by recorded votes, but that is a distinct possibility. At the very least, more congressmen would have participated, sensitive as they are to the charge of absenteeism. If they do not vote, their districts are effectively disenfranchised on each such issue; few members would want to be charged with that responsibility. Furthermore, it is common knowledge that some congressmen, on some issues, vote differently on teller votes than they do on recorded votes. Recording teller votes would allow citizens to evaluate more clearly the kind of representation they are receiving and would help insure increased responsiveness to the will of the public.

Other current suggestions with respect to committee procedures spring from the same concern with achieving a greater responsiveness on the part of Congress. These include the proposal that all committee hearings and meetings be opened to the public unless a committee, by roll call vote in open session, has decided otherwise. Committees would also be prohibited from voting to close more than one meeting at a time. Another suggestion would require that a record of all roll call votes in committees be available to the public on request, a move that would help lift the aura of secrecy surrounding committee procedures.

There are many changes which can and should be made in floor procedures. For example, House rules in the past have permitted many extremely important matters to be voted on without any debate whatsoever; in the 91st Congress this was the case with the Cooper-Church amendment dealing with funds for Cambodia. This is irrational and ought to be foreclosed by the House rules. One proposal currently under discussion is to require at least

10 minutes of debate on any motion to recommit with instructions (the form of amendment which heretofore has precluded debate) and on any amendment published in the *Congressional Record* before floor consideration. Such a change would help insure that some attention be given to motions and amendments which can drastically affect the outcome of legislation.

Similarly, it has been proposed that reports of conference committees, which have met to reconcile differences between bills on the same subject passed by the House and Senate, be printed in the *Congressional Record* at least 3 days before floor consideration and that reports be available on the floor. All too often in the past provisions which have been guided with care through one house are stricken by the conference and members are unaware of this fact when they vote to accept the compromise legislation. One of the worst examples of this was the language added to the Airport and Airways Act of 1970 forbidding the airlines to inform the traveling public of the amount of tax they are paying on their airline tickets; this change, introduced in the conference committee report, was approved by both houses before most members knew what was happening.

As with the question of seniority, many other reform provisions have been under consideration. Not all of them are wise, but the need to make the legislative process more responsive is so important that they ought to be examined. In each case, the question ought to be: will this change make the Congress more responsive to the real needs of this country as it exists in the 1970's?

THE BUSINESS OF CONGRESS

A third area in which changes are clearly needed is one of congressional housekeeping. In recent years the work of Congress has stretched on into longer and longer sessions. The handling of vital legislation, such as appropriations for all government departments, has taken progressively longer until, in some years, more than half the budget year has passed before money is appropriated to carry on vital programs. This trend needs to be reversed and could be reversed with changes in the scheduling of the work of the Congress.

The present arrangement prevents members of Congress from giving proper consideration, either in committee or on the floor, to their primary function—legislation. In fact, if someone had deliberately designed a system to frustrate the law making process, he might well have developed a system identical to the one in use today. The implications for environmental legislation are obvious; if Congress is too bogged down with routine work to get into new and tough controversies, a lot of environmental issues are going to remain in limbo.

Currently, most House committees, unlike those in the Senate, are limited to morning meetings while the House is not in session. Often, particularly early in the year, committees are forced to adjourn for routine House sessions when time could better be used for committee business. On the floor, the situation is reversed, as the House reserves afternoon hours for unneeded floor sessions early in the year, when little legislation is ready to be brought up. Toward the end of the session, the House generally restricts itself to afternoon hours when morning hours could be used as well. As a result, major and minor bills are rushed through without adequate study, or allowed to die without consideration or action, in the pressure to adjourn.

There are three possible changes which would allow better use of time and more flexibility.

First, committee work could be emphasized at the start of a congressional session and floor business in the waning months. In the beginning, committees could work full days, accompanied by brief *pro forma* House sessions for routine business which could be conducted without requiring the committees to adjourn. After two months or so, the balance could be shifted to give equal time to each. Some months later, another shift could allow members to spend most of their time in floor debate and comparatively little in committee. This schedule would enable the Congress to give adequate consideration to all legislation, including the final flood of bills from committees. Most probably such a schedule change would allow earlier adjournment than has been the case in recent years.

A second possibility would be for the House to change its weekly schedule. Instead of five mornings of committee meetings and five afternoons of floor sessions, the House could have three full days of committee work and two full days of heavy legislative business on the floor. This would allow concentration of efforts while retaining flexibility. Complex legislation could be studied in committee without interruption, and floor debate would have more continuity.

A third possibility—and this could be combined with either of the other suggested changes—would be for the House to put an end to the traditional "Tuesday-to-Thursday Club." In the past virtually all important matters have been confined to these three days of the week, allowing members to get away for weekend trips to their districts. If all five days were filled with meaningful work, few members of Congress would object to the longer week since it would mean shorter congressional sessions. Thus, they would still be able to get back to their districts to mend fences and attend to personal business, and yet at the same time Congress would be getting its work done in a more orderly fashion.

As with modifying seniority and opening the system to more scrutiny, improvement in scheduling and work patterns could make Congress much more responsive to the real needs of this country.

WHAT REFORM CAN DO

Perhaps an example from the past can put the drive for congressional reform in some perspective.

Back in the mid 1950's the House Education and Labor Committee was known as a graveyard for any kind of progressive legislation dealing with education or labor. The chairman, whose district in North Carolina had little in common with the rest of the country, held almost total control over that committee and the legislation referred to it. Then in 1959 some of the younger members of that committee organized a palace revolution and forced through new rules stripping the chairman of much of his power, giving the membership of the committee the right to schedule meetings and hearings when the chairman refused to call them, and generally infusing that committee with a healthy dose of democracy. The result was that this "graveyard of legislation" suddenly came to life. One of the first products of this reform was the Landrum-Griffin Labor Reform Act. Another was House and Senate passage of the nation's first program of general aid to education. When the House Rules Committee prevented the latter bill from going to conference to compromise differences with the Senate—thereby frustrating majorities in both houses—the stage was set for re-structuring of *that* committee at the start of the next Congress.

The movement for broad-scale congressional reform could achieve similar results for the Congress as a whole. When we consider the seriousness of the issues we are now facing— issues which affect the air we breathe, the water we drink, the reassignment of priorities to deal with the crises in our cities, questions relating to war and peace—there can be no doubt that a real effort must be made.

If the millions of Americans who feel deep concern about the future of their environment want to know where to begin, the place to start is in the makeup and organization of the Congress.

Chapter 13

How To Influence Your Congressman

by George Alderson

Each Congressman and Senator has his own interests, his own friends, each runs his own office in his own way, and each listens most attentively to a different element of his constituency. These differences are what you, a constituent, will make use of as you consider how to influence your Congressman. (Throughout this chapter we shall refer only to "Congressmen"—a term Washington hands use only for members of the House of Representatives—but the same tactics apply equally to Senators. The principal difference is that Senators are not as locally-oriented as Congressmen, and tend to take a more national viewpoint. Senate staff members also have time to go more deeply into the issues than House staff). One congressman may owe his election to labor support, so you'll want the labor unions' backing on your environmental campaign. Another may be a champion of consumer protection, so you'll be looking for consumer groups to help influence him.

Despite the differences among Congressmen,

there are many similarities, knowledge of which will aid the efforts of environmental activists throughout the country. The success of your own efforts depends on adapting the general concepts presented here to your own Congressman. You will have help from environmental lobbyists, who provide Congressmen with information on the issue and try to convert public concern into specific, effective legislation by negotiating with Congressmen. But everything lobbyists do depends on the influence you exert in your Congressional district; there is simply no substitute for the voice of the voter.

To be influential you need to seek commitments on specific measures. The failure of conservationists to do this in the past has made it possible for Congressmen to proclaim their opposition to air and water pollution year after year, without taking action on some of the worst elements of pollution. In Earth Day speeches Congressmen once again came out for clean air and water. They did not, however, commit themselves, for instance, to: (1) eliminating the internal combustion engine from automobiles by 1975, (2) stopping the supersonic transport, or (3) legalizing abortion to help stabilize the population. Until constituents get commitments from Congressmen to specific legislative principles, the environment is going to suffer.

Avoiding commitments is a Capitol Hill tradition of long standing, not an evil plot invented specifically to defeat environmental legislation. Other special interests have the same problem, but they have learned to deal with it. A noncommittal stance is so prevalent that Congressmen adopt it without thinking; in fact, it is a convenient substitute for thinking. But when a Congressman hears from his constituents forcefully asking him to take a stand, backed up with ample facts, he usually sees the value of a prompt decision.

Perhaps the best way to influence your Congressman is to influence his constituents first. Clearly, the most appropriate means for this kind of communication are the media available in your area. Local media are far more effective at affecting people's opinions than national media. For example, if people paid close attention to Huntley and Brinkley and Walter Cronkite, there would be few citizens supporting a continuation of the war in Vietnam or measures (like funding the SST) which adversely affect the environment of this country.

Almost every local area in America has some sorts of media that are produced nearby. There are small radio stations, television stations, daily newspapers, weekly journals, and small magazines. All of these are influential on local opinion. Citizens should carry their opinions and helpful information to these media in any way possible. You can:

- visit local editors and station managers personally to talk to them, encouraging coverage of important issues like ecology.
- get experts in these important fields to speak to station managers and editors. This kind of education is perhaps more important than

any speech these experts could give in the area.

have the media emphasize the local large-scale effects of proposed actions.

call radio talk shows to express opinions backed up by accurate and note-worthy facts.

try to get yourself on a local television talk show. Make sure you have done your homework before you get on the air, but also bear in mind that you are not expected to be a walking encyclopedia—but are expected to be sincerely concerned and considerate.

supply new and important books on your subject to book reviewers in your area. (Has the book you're now reading been reviewed in your local newspaper?).

Effective local media will help arouse citizen interest in working for solutions to environmental problems. Citizens will certainly want to influence their representatives in Washington to do something about the problems that are bothering them. Several courses of action are open to attempt to influence a Congressman:

THE ACTIVE LONER

Some things that influence Congressmen can be done by an individual citizen, without an organization behind him and without special pull. Done in concert, taking their cue from timely information available through environmental organizations, these tactics can be as effective as the toughest political machine.

Congressmen usually have so many issues on their hands that they leave the environment to the relevant committees of the House and simply vote for the "committee bill" when it is reported to the floor. The committee may have gutted the bill and covered its tracks with technical verbiage in the committee report; few Congressmen take the time to look into such details, so a committee is safe doing this. When Congressmen begin to pay attention to an issue, it's a different story.

On some issues, getting the Congressman's attention is enough to turn the tide. So it was with the supersonic transport plane. Until 1970, Congressmen never had to take a stand on the SST because it was never subject to a record vote in the House. But during the week before the SST appropriation reached the House floor in May 1970, a barrage of letters from constituents arrived in Congressmen's offices, triggered by conservation groups' mailings. Congressmen suddenly took an interest in the SST and began to question the committee's approval of $290 million for the project. As a result, SST opponents came within 14 votes of defeating the appropriation. This was an issue whose pros and cons were fairly obvious to Congressmen. Sentiment on the Hill was predominantly against the project, but it took constituents' letters to persuade Congressmen to give it close attention.

On most environmental issues Congressmen have little time to seek information; their chief interests lie elsewhere. Letters, therefore, serve not only as a triggering mechanism, but as an educational tool, pointing out an issue on which the Congressman can take action that will please his constituents.

THE LETTER

Letters influence a Congressman in several ways. He will not see many of the letters himself, but his staff will read them and prepare replies, frequently resorting to Robotype or printed letters when there is a large volume coming in. The Congressman will catch a glimpse of some letters when he signs the replies, and the staff will keep him informed on how the mail is running (such as, "50 letters last week against the SST; none for it"). The staff will also give him their reactions to the tone of the mail—whether it is well-reasoned and informative, or whether it is antagonistic and dictatorial. If the letters are repeating the same phrases or list of reasons, lifted from a pressure-group mailing, they will report that, too.

Staff attitudes are also important because staff members may be more receptive than the Congressman to your viewpoint. Many staffers are younger and more in touch with environmental issues than the Congressmen, and they may influence the Congressmen to act on the issue you are writing about.

No matter how you write it, your letter is going to be seen by someone at the Congressman's end who thinks, and who has more influence with him than you do. The best policy, therefore, is to write as though for someone of your own sensitivity and intelligence, who is slightly less well-informed than you are. (Don't let this list dissuade you from writing. The techniques below make for maximum effectiveness, but all letters are noted. It only takes a minute to state your position with a reason or two and send it in.) The following points will sharpen the impact of your letter:

1. Make it a page or less, covering only one subject, written in your own words, and including some thoughts of your own.
2. Refer to the bill by name and number if possible, and ask the Congressman to do something specific (such as to co-sponsor the bill).
3. Ask the Congressman to tell you his position on the matter.
4. Show your familiarity with the subject and with the current status of legislation. This will indicate that constituents are serious about the environment, unlike the casual, uninformed correspondents who produce much constituent mail.
5. Give reasons for your position. Cite your own experience and observations if possible. Mentioning the bill's impact on the Congressman's district makes it a local issue, easier for a Congressman to respond to.
6. Don't mention your membership in environmental groups. Congressmen usually know the organization's position already. The individual citizen's letter is what counts, not the letter obviously inspired by an organization.
7. If you can, cite the Congressman's vote on a recent issue to show your awareness of his record. For example: "I was sorry to learn that you voted for the SST, but

I hope you will be supporting the Environmental Protection Act."
8. Ask a question you would like the Congressman to answer.

In general, be helpful rather than threatening. Congressmen get enough crackpot mail, too little that offers to lend a hand. The best threat is the unvoiced one that consists of a pile of thoughtful letters asking the Congressman to take a stand; he knows that the writers are going to be voting in the next election. You can best show your sincerity not by threatening to campaign against him, but by offering to provide further information on the subject of your letter. The attitude will pay off, even though your offer may never be taken up.

The Follow-up Letter

Sooner or later the Congressman will reply. What you do now will further separate the serious constituent from the casual one. Mass mailings can stimulate a respectable batch of mail to a Congressman, but they can't stimulate follow-up letters.

If the Congressman agrees with you, this is your chance to compliment him and ask him to take an active role in the campaign, instead of merely waiting for the bill to come to a vote on the floor. He can influence his colleagues in Congress and help generate more public support for his position by co-sponsoring the bill, by testifying when the relevant committee holds hearings, by talking to committee members who are considering the issue, and by making speeches and writing articles for public consumption. Get him to commit himself publicly, if he hasn't already.

If the Congressman is noncommittal, you have a chance to write and give him more reasons for your stand. Point out that he failed to indicate his position, and request a more responsive answer. Sometimes a Congressman may have a legitimate reason for remaining uncommitted. A few Congressmen make a fetish of remaining uncommitted until the floor debate —some for intellectual reasons, others to be able to trade their votes to Congressmen from whom they will need favors later on. But if your letter is directed to a specific principle, rather than to a large and complex subject area, you are entitled to a good answer from your Congressman.

If the Congressman disagrees with you, you can respond with a rebuttal to his arguments. If he gives no reasons for his stand, you can ask him to explain himself. Bear in mind that even thoroughly committed Congressmen change their minds when enough constituents request it. In politics nothing is forever.

Telegrams

Because a telegram generally is shorter and contains less reasoning than a letter, it has different uses. The most effective use of the telegram is in the last few days before a vote, when you want to remind the Congressman that his constituents are still aware of the issue and are interested in how he votes. You can send a Personal Opinion Message of 15 words to your Congressman or Senator via Western Union for 90¢ anywhere in the country.

As long as House procedure prohibits record votes on most crucial amendments, it will be necessary to urge your Congressman to be on the floor to vote. Many crucial amendments have lost because too many Congressmen who supported them were in their offices instead of on the floor. Telegrams can be helpful in this regard, if you follow up with a letter inquiring whether he did vote, and how.

Some Congressmen who did not vote may write to constituents: "I supported the amendment," without mentioning that they did not actually *vote* for it. This ploy is partly a result of the non-record vote, but it is also a result of inadequate coverage of the House by newspapers. The principal solution is to urge your local papers to have their Washington correspondents cover the environmental actions of your Congressman in depth, instead of relying on the wire service stories, which are too general to tell much of significance about local Congressmen. Some papers already do this well; most don't.

Letters to the Editor

The letters column of a newspaper offers an opportunity to communicate with your Congressman in public. The Congressman rarely will answer, but your printed letter will get more of his attention and may also stimulate others to write him. The well-written one-page letter is the basic weapon in this case. Instead of writing to the Congressman, you write to the editor, commenting on the Congressman's stand.

The best way to break into the letters column is to cite a recent editorial or news item related to your subject. If the Congressman has commented publicly on your subject, you're ready to go. If not, try the indirect approach. For example, if the Congressman has been proud of his efforts to cut government spending, you point out the irony of his failure to oppose the $290-million SST appropriation. Inconsistencies always seem to have news value.

If the Congressman does something good on your issue, don't lose the chance to do him a favor by praising him in the letters column. In this case, send him a carbon copy so he'll see it even if the paper doesn't print it. Reciprocity is a principle Congressmen believe in and apply constantly; take advantage of it when you can.

Editors also accept letters not tied directly to recent newspaper coverage. A good, new idea, well-presented, usually ranks above the routine complaints about typographical errors and bad grammar. Editors look for news value and good expression.

Beware, however, of writing to the same paper too often. The crackpot threshold is lower here than in the regular mail to a Congressman, and you need to avoid seeming to be interested chiefly in making the Congressman look good or bad. The emphasis has to be on the issues. If you've had a letter in one newspaper recently and you want to write another one, either send it to a different paper or ghost it for a friend to sign.

Letters to the editor will have their impact even if they never see print, because they show the editor that readers are interested in your subject. The results may include editorials and more thorough coverage in the news columns. The Washington bureaus of several newspapers and wire services include reporters who are excellent in covering environmental issues, but whose editors insist that they minimize the time spent on environment stories, on grounds that readers are not interested.

Visiting the Congressman

When you have the facts down cold, ask the Congressman for an appointment to see him when he visits the district. Most Congressmen whose seats are not absolutely safe spend as much time as they can in their districts, meeting constituents and speaking to organizations. They are thus able to keep constituents aware of their names and faces, and to find out what constituents are interested in.

Eastern Congressmen often go home every weekend, those from the Midwest and the West Coast at least once every few weeks. Each maintains a district office. (A Senator maintains an office in one or two principal cities of his state.) You can arrange an appointment either through the local office or through the Washington office. Senators' and Congressmen's Washington offices can be reached by telephone through the U. S. Capitol switchboard, (202) 224-3121.

If you're uneasy about seeing the Congressman on your own (afraid of forgetting the arguments, or of showing your anger if he should seem irrational, look for a neighbor or colleague who shares your interest, and see the Congressman together.

When in Washington, make a point of dropping in to see the Congressman. He will usually be more available to constituents in Washington than in the crowded schedule of his district visits. An informed and interested constituent can always do more to win a Congressman over than a raft of Washington lobbyists without district connections.

THE ORGANIZER

Plenty of organizations want to help the environment, but don't know the issues. If you know the facts of your issue, you have something to offer them—information—in exchange for their support.

Many an environmental measure has languished simply for lack of organizers to do the cheerleading, to gather the allies and advise them when and how to use their influence. An organizer need not be a pillar of any existing organization, although it helps to know a few leaders of local groups.

If you begin organizing things on your issue, you'll find that as the effort broadens, help will begin coming in from sources you never knew existed. It may be a hard push at first, but after a while the campaign acquires a life of its own, reaching into the nooks and crannies of the Congressional district.

Organizations

Congressmen are highly sensitive to organized opinion, especially when it represents a broad spectrum of constituents and appears to be serious.

In seeking allies it is always helpful to have one or two of the well-known national environmental groups, or their local affiliates, on your side, because their endorsement is a credential that reassures other groups that it's a *bona fide* environmental issue. Then go after all the other groups you know locally that can take a stand on the issue. When an organization takes a stand, ask its leaders to publicize the stand in the newspapers and let the Congressmen know. As you work on the issue, you'll develop contacts that can approach the other groups more influentially than you can, and so your campaign broadens.

The more unexpected the source, the more valuable its support will be. Congressmen expect the Sierra Club and Friends of the Earth to be defending the environment, but when they begin hearing from the PTA, the Machinists' Union, and the American Federation of Teachers, they'll think twice about the issue.

Organizational support can often be mustered through a local coalition, involving a variety of groups that endorse a single policy objective. The Massachusetts Committee Against the SST, for example, included several statewide organizations that opposed funding for the supersonic transport. Formation of the Committee was a newsworthy event, covered in the Boston papers, and the Committee served as a rallying point for the efforts of participating organizations as they campaigned for the votes of Massachusetts Congressmen. A similar coalition was formed in Cleveland, Ohio. Both coalitions obtained dramatic results, including the reversal of the positions of Congressmen closely involved in the SST issue.

Publicity created by local coalitions, and by independent organizations, helps to make a national issue more newsworthy to the local papers, and generates a bandwagon effect among citizens and organizations.

Some organizations like publicity. Others don't, and would rather limit their participation to sending a telegram to the Congressman. As an organizer you help each group do whatever it can.

Politicians

Congressmen pay attention to what state and local politicians are saying in public, because these people supposedly hear more directly from the people than the Congressman 1000 miles away in Washington. Many of these politicians are accessible and eager for good publicity on environmental matters because they are on the way up, looking for popular issues that distinguish them from the entrenched officeholders. This is true of Democrats and Republicans alike, including mayors, county executives, state legislators and even governors. Working with them on environmental issues enables you to get acquainted with the powers of the future, and at the same time to influence the incumbent Congressman.

What you want here is chiefly publicity, to stimulate general awareness of the issue as a political decision. Among the possibilities get him to: make a speech on the issue, testify when Congress holds hearings, hold a press conference (perhaps involving other local politicians as well), or send the Congressman a letter and release the text to the press. You'll need to plan tactics that will work in your own situation, because a lot depends on the newsworthiness of the politician and of what you get him to do. By using a little ingenuity you can undoubtedly find new approaches that will be effective.

The election opponent of a Congressman, either in the primary or in the general election, may be delighted to take a stand if the Congressman hasn't, or if the Congressman took the wrong position. To have his anti-environmental stand challenged in a campaign frequently forces a Congressman to change his mind. If it doesn't, it will influence his stand on future environmental issues. This is so valuable a tactic that it is worth a good deal of time to set it up. Campaign contributors generally provide the best access. The candidate will want facts on the issue and solid evidence of the Congressman's stand, including what the

Congressman said that may be quotable, and how he voted.

Young Democrats and Young Republicans can also effectively take a stand on environmental issues. Incumbent Congressmen tend not to be very influential with the YDs and YRs, yet the young politicians by expressing a consensus can help influence the Congressmen. The youth wing of the party is usually eager to prove that it can respond to modern concerns, thus dispelling the old-guard image of the incumbents.

Citizen Uprising

The aim of all this is to get environmental issues out of the academic cloisters and into public life. Because Congressmen are in the habit of responding to the interests of their constituents, you need to get the constituents interested. The broader a cross-section of the district you can involve, the harder it is for the Congressman to ignore. When you get the backing of the voters he needs most—the swing precincts that he can't quite count on, and the contributors to his campaign funds—then you're learning how to influence your Congressman.

Chapter 14

Become a Lobbyist for the Environment

by Garrett De Bell

You pay the salaries of the oil lobby every time you buy a gallon of gas. Whether you want to support their policies or not, you are paying the salaries of the lobbyists who work for the Alaska pipeline, offshore oil drilling, more highways, more and bigger supertankers, and the other policies that perpetuate the overemphasis on the smog-producing and excessively dangerous automobile. If you want to be part of the solution as well as part of the problem, you will have to take the responsibility for funding groups which are lobbying for ecologically sound policy. Unfortunately, most people from high school and college students to retired people have money for a dinner in a restaurant or an occasional movie but don't have a paying membership in even one effective conservation organization. A good bandwagon to jump on would be the growing trend of giving your friends memberships in groups such as Friends of the Earth, John Muir Institute, Zero Population Growth, Environmental Action, and Sierra Club.

This is a painless way to donate money and support your share of the environmental movement while at the same time ending your support of the unnecessary production and consumption of "goods" in the Christmas Season (Only thirty more BUYING days till Christmas). This pitch for money is necessary because of the human quirk that people are willing to pay for material possessions that are clearly related to the payment while not being willing to make the much more necessary investment in organizations that will increase the likelihood of a future.

Lobbying is one important way conservation organizations influence policy that affects the quality of the environment. Most people don't have a clear idea of what lobbyists do. They think that lobbying is some sort of unethical action by the representatives of polluting industries; the connotation is of bribes, influence peddling and so forth. This is a fatal misconception. The only thing wrong with lobbying is that only the interests that have money to spend are adequately represented. The oil, automobile, steel, aero-space and other interests can spend a small per cent of their profit to fund a more than adequate Washington office with lobbyists, research staffs, back-up support and so on.

Lobbying is simply trying to influence legislators to back legislation that is supported by the organization the lobbyist represents. The techniques are varied, but primarily involve getting arguments researched and presented in such a way as would most effectively demonstrate to a congressman that a certain position is in his constituents' interest and his career will be aided by his taking the position you advocate. The main effort of a lobbyist is getting all the information that supports your position to all congressmen who might be persuaded to vote your way. Boeing gets the pro arguments for the SST to Congress. Friends of the Earth, Zero Population Growth, Sierra Club, and Environmental Action tell Congress the other side of the story. A lobbyist spends a lot of time helping congressmen who are already on your side of the issue to increase their effectiveness. This help takes the form of writing speeches and articles about your issue for the representative to use, getting him specific facts and examples to use in influencing his colleagues to change to your position, getting him information on which congressmen he is most likely to be able to influence by presenting your arguments to them, spending enough time with him and his staff to convince him of the need to give your issue priority over less pressing ones, and giving him assistance of any type needed if he is leading a fight on a particular bill or is a major sponsor of legislation you favor. With representatives who are uncommitted to either side of an issue, the tactic is to spend enough time with the congressman and, more importantly, with his aides to convince him of the advantage to him, his constituents, and the country of supporting your cause. It is always implicit that voting the wrong way on critical issues may result in bad publicity in his district and your group's support of his opponent in the next election. With the hard core opposition lobbyists can do little. The main effort there should be to help find good candidates to unseat the representative in the next election.

The main need is to equalize the balance of power by getting more lobbyists (and other full time staff) working for ecologically sound policy. Your memberships paid to the above groups are the source of salaries and expenses for eco-lobbyists and for necessary research and education.

In addition to financially supporting the efforts of lobbyists and others working for the organizations you belong to, you can individually be much more effective in influencing the system if you learn how it works. You can be a lobbyist for the environment. The information a lobbyist learns in his first week is enough to multiply your effectiveness many times over if you will take the time to acquire it. Your local chapter of any environment group can become increasingly more effective as soon as one or a few members learn how the system works, how to get up-to-date information on legislation as it is amended, changed, locked up in committee and find where and when the groups' influence can be used to good advantage.

Most Americans are, unfortunately, very naïve about the workings of the government and how it can be influenced. No American corporations share this naïvete. They know who makes decisions in areas they are concerned with, they know how to get every argument in favor of a policy they support to all the people who need to be influenced. If we are to counter their efforts, we must do the homework, learn how the system works and then change it.

The following short list is our suggestion for a do-it-yourself lobbyist kit. Any group and many individuals can afford to establish a reading shelf with these books and periodicals.

DO-IT-YOURSELF LOBBYIST KIT

Five books that give a good clear view of how Congress works and the pressures and influences on your congressman; every concerned citizen should read at least one of these books:

THE HOUSE OF REPRESENTATIVES

Clem Miller, *Member of the House: Letters of a Congressman,* New York, Scribner's, 1962, $2.95.

Donald G. Tacheron and Morris K. Udall (Member of Congress from Arizona), *The Job of the Congressman,* Indianapolis, Bobbs-Merrill Co., 1966, $6.50 (hardcover), $2.75 (paper).

Charles E. Clapp, *The Congressman: His Work as He Sees It,* Washington, D.C., The Brookings Institute, 1963, $6.00.

THE SENATE
Donald R. Matthews, *U.S. Senators and Their World,* University of North Carolina Press, Chapel Hill, 1960, $6.00 (hardcover), $1.95 (paper, Vin. Random).

LOBBYING
Lewis Anthony Dexter, *How Organizations are Represented in Washington,* Indianapolis, Bobbs-Merrill Co., 1969, $6.75 (hardcover), $2.95 (paper).
A good short treatment of how lobbying works and how organizations work to influence Congress and the Executive Branch of the Federal Government.

CURRENT INFORMATION ON CONGRESSIONAL ACTION
Congressional Record, $1.50 a month to Supt. of Documents, Government Printing Office, Washington, D.C. 20402. A complete record of all the previous day's action in the Congress, published daily. The daily digest at the back of each day's *Congressional Record* summarizes all of the previous day's floor and committee action and indexes this to the main text of the record. One person skimming the *Record* can keep the whole organization informed of the progress of key bills. Also, most new ideas and good magazine and newspaper articles on ecology are entered by some representative in the *Congressional Record* so it is a good source of information.

BECOME A LOBBYIST FOR THE ENVIRONMENT

Sierra Club National News Report, available at $12 a year. Sierra Club, 1050 Mills Tower, San Francisco, California 94104. This is a two page summary of Capitol Hill news with up-to-date information on Federal decisions that affect the environment. It is published weekly when Congress is in session and is mailed first class so you get it fast enough to act upon this information.

REFERENCES

Congressional Directory
GPO Washington, D.C. 20402 $4, $4.50 thumb indexed
Lists all the different committee assignments of congressmen, includes biographical information of the congressmen to give you some idea of their background and other interests.

Congressional Staff Directory $12.50
Write to: Congressional Staff Directory
300 New Jersey Avenue S.E., Washington, D.C. 20003
Includes committee assignments and also subcommittee assignments and is most useful in its lists of the staff members of Congress and of all congressional committees. Biographies of both congressional and committee staff are included to give you some help in finding staff aides whom you might have easier access to. One of the first things a lobbyist learns in Washington is that it is more important to get to key staff people than to the congressman

himself because the staff have time to consider all your arguments and if you can convince them, they will get your argument to the congressman.

YOUR CONGRESSMAN'S PERFORMANCE

The Friends of the Earth chart on how your congressmen vote on critical environmental issues, reprinted in this book, is available as a wall chart at 50¢ from Friends of the Earth, 917 15th Street N.W., Washington, D.C. 20005. Evaluations of congressmen are done by many other organizations and you would do well to get the ones from any organization which you feel represents your interests. All of these voting record analyses must be used with discretion because of the problems, discussed in the chapters on Congress in this book, that many key votes are not recorded and congressmen often change their vote when they know it will be recorded as a roll call vote. Hopefully, the bill now in progress to require all votes to be recorded as roll call votes will pass before the end of this Congress so you can know your congressman's position more fully.

COMMITTEE ASSIGNMENTS

The names of congressmen assigned to each committee and subcommittee can be obtained as a free one-page pamphlet from the chairman of each committee. If you don't have the *Congressional Staff Directory,* you should write for the list of subcommittee assignments. To be effective in influencing ecologically sound legislation you must know your congressman's committee and sub-committee assignment so that your group can use their influence to get your congressman to work for the kind of bills you want whenever relevant legislation is in his subcommittee because committees and subcommittees are the easiest place to change bills.

A FEW HINTS FOR EFFECTIVE LOBBYING

The best way to start out your efforts to lobby for the environment is pick an issue that particularly concerns you, read up on the substance of the issue, and then start keeping track of possible legislative approaches, existing bills, their progress and the effect of citizen and industry campaigns to modify the bill. By trying to influence policy in one area and learning the specifics involved, you will soon know how to be effective in other areas. One person with thorough understanding of an ecological issue, its progress in congress, his congressman's positions on it and related issues can be incredibly effective by attending talks given by the representative in the district and forcing him to defend his position to his constituents. The common practice of big talk and no action cannot survive an educated electorate. Either the representative's position and action will change (as did the position of many representatives on the SST issue where the environment lost by 64 votes in November 1969 and only 14 votes in May 1970) or the citizens will become aware of the representative's true position, find a new candidate and replace the incumbent with an ecologically sound congressman. A few citizens can have a tremendous impact.

Your local conservation group should consider raising the funds needed to send one of your members to Washington to gain some firsthand experience by working with lobbying organizations like Friends of the Earth, Zero Population Growth, Environmental Action, and Sierra Club, with related groups like the Center for the Study of Responsive Law (Ralph Nader's organization which researches and exposes the workings of the government agencies) or as a temporary assistant to a congressman or Senator. Firsthand experience by a few of your members will increase your group's effectiveness considerably.

The conclusion of this section, this book, and every statement on environmental policy or politics is the same. It is up to you; you must become informed and involved. It's been said a million times but it's still true that democracy only works if the electorate is informed and politically active.

IT'S UP TO YOU.

DO IT YOURSELF.

GIVE MONEY TO ENVIRONMENTAL GROUPS SO THEY CAN REPRESENT YOUR INTERESTS.

(Membership applications and brief statements of purposes appear in the back of the book.)

ORGANIZATIONS WITH ACTIVE LOBBYING EFFORTS

Friends of the Earth
30 East 42nd Street
New York, N.Y. 10017

General Membership $15, Spouse $5, Student $5, Supporting $25, Contributing $50, Life $250

Zero Population Growth
330 Second Street
Los Altos, California 94022

General Membership $10 Student $4 Donor $20 Patron $120

Environmental Action
2000 P Street N.W.
Washington, D.C. 20036

Sierra Club
1050 Mills Tower
San Francisco, California 94104

THE CONGRESS AND FEDERAL AGENCIES

Center for the Study of Responsive Law
1908 Q Street N.W.
Washington, D.C. 20009

Ralph Nader's incredibly effective research and action team in Washington which has places for about 100 fulltime "Nader's Raiders" each summer and a small fulltime staff the rest of the year.

In addition to the action groups which are stressed above, many other more general groups are concerned with conservation, environment, and population. The other conservation groups which do some lobbying on certain issues are primarily involved with land purchase or popular education and are listed below.

Scientists' Institute for Public Information
30 E. 68th Street
New York, New York 10021
(212) 249-2886

The Nature Conservancy
1522 K Street, N.W.
Washington, D.C. 20005
(202) 223-4710

The National Wildlife Federation
1412 16th Street, N.W.
Washington, D.C. 20036
(202) 232-8004

National Audubon Society
1130 Fifth Avenue
New York, New York 10028
(212) 369-2100

The Conservation Foundation
1250 Connecticut Avenue, N.W.
Washington, D.C. 20036
(202) 659-2180

The Wilderness Society
729 15th Street, N.W.
Washington, D.C. 20005
(202) 347-4132

National Parks Association
1701 18th Street, N.W.
Washington, D.C. 20009
(202) 667-3352

International Union for Conservation Of Nature and Natural Resources
2000 P Street, N.W.
Washington, D.C. 20006

The Izaak Walton League of America
1326 Waukegan Road
Glenview, Illinois 60025
(312) 724-3880

John Muir Institute for Environmental Studies
451 Pacific Avenue
San Francisco, California 94133
Or, P.O. Box 11
Cedar Crest, New Mexico 87008

Citizens League Against the Sonic Boom
19 Appleton Street
Cowbridge, Massachusetts 02138

Planned Parenthood/World Population
515 Madison Avenue
New York, New York 10022

There are a great many organizations which are not primarily environmental which you may already belong to. It would be very worthwhile to attempt to convince these groups of the importance of the environmental issues and political action to their basic purpose and use them to set up environmental sections or committees. Many groups that are not primarily concerned with the environment, from consumer groups to labor unions, helped in the SST fight.

Chapter 15

Understanding Congressional Voting Records

by Richard H. Meeker

This chapter consists of congressional voting records. Two listings are offered. The first is the Friends of the Earth analysis of 10 key environmental issues in the House of Representatives since 1960. The second list is prepared by the Society of Friends Committee on National Legislation. It is a more general sampling of key votes by your Representatives and Senators in last year's session of Congress.

These lists do not tell as much as they should. For instance, many significant votes in both houses of Congress are not roll call votes (an individual's name is not recorded with his vote), making it hard to tell who voted for or against certain pieces of legislation. At the same time, many bills are greatly altered in committee before being voted on by Congress. It takes a committee vote to approve a bill for discussion on the floor of one of the houses of Congress. These votes, as well as the discussions which lead up to them, are not generally released to the public by committee chairmen. Most people in this country have not even heard of the Committee of the Whole House, which considers amendments to bills before they are brought to the floor of the House. No vote in this "committee" is ever recorded, though an affirmative vote leads to a floor vote.

Some congressmen heartily approve of all this secrecy, for it allows them to have "clean" voting records while remaining antagonistic to the environment in committee and in their many votes that remain unrecorded. Each citizen's power of the ballot is greatly diminished, because he lacks full information about the voting records of his elected representatives. This is why congressional rules must be changed so that in the future all votes in House and Senate subcommittee and full committee, the Committee of the Whole House, the House of Representatives, and the Senate of the United States of America must be publicly recorded role call votes. This will help make the votes of congressmen consistent with their high-minded public statements.

In spite of these drawbacks, the voting records presented here are the best available indicators of performance. They make it clear that congressmen generally follow the same beliefs and interest groups on every issue.

On each piece of legislation, Friends of the Earth and the Society of Friends preferred one vote over another. The preferred votes are indicated by black boxes, while the less satisfactory votes are indicated by white boxes.

HOW YOUR CONGRESSMAN VOTED ON CRITICAL ENVIRONMENTAL ISSUES

Evaluated by the League of Conservation Voters in cooperation with Friends of the Earth

■ = for the environment   ☐ = unfavorable
▨ = Absent   — = Not yet in Congress

1. Indirect vote on the SST. A "no" vote would have allowed an amendment to the recommittal motion to delete all funds for supersonic transport. (Passed, 176-162. 1970, HR 17755. A "no" vote is a vote for the environment.)
no = ■

2. Vote on whether to grant a rule for the Timber Supply Bill, which would have increased the logging on national forests. (Defeated, 150-228. 1970, HR 12025. A "no" vote is for conservation.)
no = ■

3. Indirect vote for $1 billion clean water appropriation. A "no" vote would have allowed an amendment to the public works appropriation bill to spend $1 billion. (Passed 215-187. 1969, HR 14159. A "no" vote is against pollution.)
no = ■

4. Vote to recommit bill creating the San Rafael Wilderness Area. Conservationists voted "yes" for recommittal, because the proposed boundaries in the bill were much too small. (Defeated, 156-238. 1968, S 889.)

yes=

5. Vote to recommit mass transportation act with instructions to limit authorizations to $150 million in 1968, instead of $175 million a year after 1967. (Passed, 205-160. 1966, HR 14810. A "no" vote is for mass transit.)

no=

6. Bill authorizing the Secretary of Interior to preserve estuarine areas. (Suspension of rules, requiring a 2/3 majority; failed 209-108. A "yes" vote is for conservation. 1966, HR 13447.)

yes=

7. Vote to accept Rep. Udall's definition of the boundaries for the Indiana Dunes National Lakeshore. (Passed 183-147. 1966, HR 51. A "yes" vote is for parks.)

yes=

UNDERSTANDING CONGRESSIONAL VOTING RECORDS   215

8. Vote to recommit Clean Air Act with instructions to delete Title II for research on solid waste disposal. (Defeated 80-220. 1965, S 306. A "no" vote is against pollution.)

no = ▇

9. Amendment to the Public Works Appropriation Bill to reduce funds for several Army Corps of Engineers construction projects, including the cross-Florida barge canal. (Defeated 84-120. 1962, HR 12900. A "yes" vote is for conservation.)

yes = ▇

10. Vote to recommit the Water Pollution Control Bill, with instructions to reduce the annual authorization for sewage treatment grants to communities from $100 million per year, to $75 million per year. (Defeated, 165-256. A "no" vote is against pollution. 1961, HR 6441.)

no = ▇

Abbitt, Watkins M.	Virginia								
Abernethy, Thomas G.	Mississippi								
Adair, E. Ross	Indiana								
Adams, Brock	Washington								
Addabbo, Joseph P.	New York								
Albert, Carl	Oklahoma								
Alexander, Bill	Arkansas								
Anderson, Glenn M.	California								
Anderson, John B.	Illinois								
Anderson, William R.	Tennessee								
Andrews, George	Alabama								
Andrews, Mark	North Dakota								
Annunzio, Frank	Illinois								
Arends, Leslie C.	Illinois								
Ashbrook, John M.	Ohio								
Ashley, Thomas L.	Ohio								
Aspinall, Wayne N.	Colorado								
Ayres, William H.	Ohio								
Baring, Walter S.	Nevada								
Barrett, William A.	Pennsylvania								
Beall, J. Glenn, Jr.	Maryland								
Belcher, Page	Oklahoma								
Bell, Alphonzo	California								
Bennett, Charles E.	Florida								
Berry, E. Y.	South Dakota								
Betts, Jackson E.	Ohio								

Bevill, Tom	Alabama										
Biaggi, Mario	New York										
Biester, Edward G., Jr.	Pennsylvania										
Bingham, Jonathan B.	New York										
Blackburn, Benjamin B.	Georgia										
Blanton, Ray	Tennessee										
Blatnik, John A.	Minnesota										
Boggs, Hale	Louisiana										
Boland, Edward P.	Massachusetts										
Bolling, Richard	Missouri										
Bow, Frank T.	Ohio										
Brademas, John	Indiana										
Brasco, Frank J.	New York										
Bray, William G.	Indiana										
Brinkley, Jack	Georgia										
Brock, William E, III	Tennessee										
Brooks, Jack	Texas										
Broomfield, William S.	Michigan										
Brotzman, Donald G.	Colorado										
Brown, Clarence J.	Ohio										
Brown, Garry	Michigan										
Brown, George E., Jr.	California										
Broyhill, James T.	North Carolina										
Broyhill, Joel T.	Virginia										
Buchanan, John	Alabama										
Burke, J. Herbert	Florida										

Burke, James A.	Massachusetts											
Burleson, Omar	Texas											
Burlison, Bill D.	Missouri											
Burton, Laurence J.	Utah											
Burton, Phillip	California											
Bush, George	Texas											
Button, Daniel E.	New York											
Byrne, James A.	Pennsylvania											
Byrnes, John W.	Wisconsin											
Cabell, Earle	Texas											
Caffery, Patrick T.	Louisiana											
Camp, John N.	Oklahoma											
Carey, Hugh L.	New York											
Carter, Tim L.	Kentucky											
Casey, Bob	Texas											
Cederberg, Elford A.	Michigan											
Celler, Emanuel	New York											
Chamberlain, Charles E.	Michigan											
Chappell, Bill, Jr.	Florida											
Chisholm, Shirley	New York											
Clancy, Donald D.	Ohio											
Clark, Frank M.	Pennsylvania											
Clausen, Don H.	California											
Clawson, Del	California											
Clay, William	Missouri											
Cleveland, James C.	New Hampshire											

Cohelan, Jeffery	California									
Collier, Harold R.	Illinois									
Collins, James M.	Texas									
Colmer, William M.	Mississippi									
Conable, Barber B., Jr.	New York									
Conte, Silvio O.	Massachusetts									
Conyers, John, Jr.	Michigan									
Corbett, Robert J.	Pennsylvania									
Corman, James C.	Iowa									
Coughlin, R. Lawrence	Pennsylvania									
Cowger, William C.	Kentucky									
Cramer, William C.	Florida									
Crane, Philip M.	Illinois									
Culver, John C.	Iowa									
Cunningham, Glenn	Nebraska									
Daddario, Emilio Q.	Connecticut									
Daniel, W. C.	Virginia									
Daniels, Dominick V.	New Jersey									
Davis, Glenn R.	Wisconsin									
Davis, John W.	Georgia									
Dawson, William L.	Illinois									
De La Garza, Eligio	Texas									
Delaney, James J.	New York									
Dellenback, John	Oregon									
Denney, Robert V.	Nebraska									
Dennis, David W.	Indiana									

Dent, John H.	Pennsylvania									
Derwinski, Edward J.	Illinois									
Devine, Samuel L.	Ohio									
Dickinson, William L.	Alabama									
Diggs, Charles C., Jr.	Michigan									
Dingell, John D.	Michigan									
Donohue, Harold D.	Massachusetts									
Dorn, Wm. J. B.	South Carolina									
Dowdy, John	Texas									
Downing, Thomas N.	Virginia									
Dulski, Thaddeus J.	New York									
Duncan, John J.	Tennessee									
Dwyer, Florence P.	New Jersey									
Eckhardt, Bob	Texas									
Edmondson, Ed	Oklahoma									
Edwards, Don	California									
Edwards, Edwin W.	Louisiana									
Edwards, Jack	Alabama									
Eilberg, Joshua	Pennsylvania									
Erlenborn, John N.	Illinois									
Esch, Marvin	Michigan									
Eshleman, Edwin D.	Pennsylvania									
Evans, Frank E.	Colorado									
Evins, Joe L.	Tennessee									
Fallon, George H.	Maryland									
Farbstein, Leonard	New York									

Fascell, Dante B.	Florida	▨	■	■	■	■	■	■	■	■	▨	■
Feighan, Michael A.	Ohio	▨	■	□	■	■	■	■	■	■	▨	■
Findley, Paul	Illinois	□	■	■	□	□	□	■	□	□	□	▨
Fish, Hamilton, Jr.	New York	■	■	■	□	□	■	■	■	■	·	·
Fisher, O. C.	Texas	□	■	□	□	□	■	□	▨	■	·	·
Flood, Daniel J.	Pennsylvania	□	■	■	□	□	■	■	▨	▨	·	·
Flowers, Walter	Alabama	·	□	□	□	□	■	■	□	·	·	·
Flynt, John J., Jr.	Georgia	□	■	□	□	□	■	▨	■	■	□	□
Foley, Thomas S.	Washington	▨	■	■	■	■	■	▨	■	▨	·	□
Ford, Gerald R.	Michigan	·	■	■	■	■	■	■	■	■	·	·
Ford, William D.	Michigan	■	■	■	■	■	■	■	■	■	·	■
Foreman, Ed	New Mexico	·	▨	□	·	□	·	□	·	·	·	·
Fountain, L. H.	North Carolina	□	■	□	□	□	■	□	■	■	□	□
Fraser, Donald M.	Minnesota	▨	■	■	■	■	■	■	■	■	▨	■
Frelinghuysen, Peter	New Jersey	■	□	■	□	▨	▨	■	▨	▨	▨	□
Frey, Louis, Jr.	Florida	▨	■	□	□	·	·	■	·	·	·	·
Friedel, Samuel N.	Maryland	·	■	□	□	□	■	■	▨	■	·	■
Fulton, James G.	Pennsylvania	□	■	■	■	□	■	■	▨	▨	▨	■
Fulton, Richard	Tennessee	□	■	□	□	□	■	■	■	■	■	■
Fuqua, Don	Florida	□	■	□	□	□	■	□	□	□	□	□
Galifianakis, Nick	North Carolina	□	■	□	□	□	■	■	■	▨	□	■
Gallagher, Cornelius E.	New Jersey	▨	■	■	■	■	■	■	■	▨	▨	■
Garmatz, Edward A.	Maryland	·	■	□	□	□	■	▨	▨	▨	▨	·
Gaydos, Joseph M.	Pennsylvania	▨	■	□	□	·	■	■	■	■	·	·
Gettys, Tom S.	South Carolina	□	■	□	□	□	□	▨	□	■	·	·
Giaimo, Robert N.	Connecticut	■	■	□	■	▨	■	■	■	▨	▨	■

Gibbons, Sam	Florida										
Gilbert, Jacob H.	New York										
Goldwater, Barry M., Jr.	California										
Gonzalez, Henry B.	Texas										
Goodling, George A.	Pennsylvania										
Gray, Kenneth J.	Illinois										
Green, Edith	Oregon										
Green, William J.	Pennsylvania										
Griffin, Charles	Mississippi										
Griffiths, Martha W.	Michigan										
Gross, H. R.	Iowa										
Grover, James R., Jr.	New York										
Gubser, Charles S.	California										
Gude, Gilbert	Maryland										
Hagan, G. Elliott	Georgia										
Haley, James A.	Florida										
Hall, Durward G.	Missouri										
Halpern, Seymour	New York										
Hamilton, Lee H.	Indiana										
Hammerschmidt, J. P.	Arkansas										
Hanley, James M.	New York										
Hanna, Richard T.	California										
Hansen, Julia Butler	Washington										
Hansen, Orval	Idaho										
Harrington, Michael	Massachusetts										
Harsha, William H.	Ohio										

Harvey, James	Michigan											
Hastings, James F.	New York											
Hathaway, William D.	Maine											
Hawkins, Augustus F.	California											
Hays, Wayne L.	Ohio											
Hebert, F. Edward	Louisiana											
Hechler, Ken	West Virginia											
Heckler, Margaret M.	Massachusetts											
Helstoski, Henry	New Jersey											
Henderson, David N.	North Carolina											
Hicks, Floyd V.	Washington											
Hogan, Lawrence J.	Maryland											
Holifield, Chet	California											
Horton, Frank	New York											
Hosmer, Craig	California											
Howard, James J.	New Jersey											
Hull, W. R., Jr.	Missouri											
Hungate, William L.	Missouri											
Hunt, John E.	New Jersey											
Hutchinson, Edward	Michigan											
Ichord, Richard H.	Missouri											
Jacobs, Andrew, Jr.	Indiana											
Jarman, John	Oklahoma											
Johnson, Albert W.	Pennsylvania											
Johnson, Harold T.	California											
Jonas, Charles	North Carolina											

Jones, Ed.	Tennessee									
Jones, Robert E.	Alabama									
Jones, Walter B.	North Carolina									
Karth, Joseph E.	Minnesota									
Kastenmeier, Robert	Wisconsin									
Kazen, Abraham, Jr.	Texas									
Kee, James	West Virginia									
Keith, Hastings	Massachusetts									
King, Carleton J.	New York									
Kleppe, Thomas S.	North Dakota									
Kluczynski, John C.	Illinois									
Koch, Edward I.	New York									
Kuykendall, Dan	Tennessee									
Kyl, John	Iowa									
Kyros, Peter N.	Maine									
Landgrebe, Earl F.	Indiana									
Landrum, Phil M.	Georgia									
Langen, Odin	Minnesota									
Latta, Delbert L.	Ohio									
Leggett, Robert L.	California									
Lennon, Alton	North Carolina									
Lloyd, Sherman P.	Utah									
Long, Clarence D.	Maryland									
Long, Speedy	Louisiana									
Lowenstein, Allard K.	New York									
Lujan, Manuel, Jr.	New Mexico									

Lukens, Donald E.	Ohio										
McCarthy, Richard D.	New York										
McClory, Robert	Illinois										
McCloskey, Paul N., Jr.	California										
McClure, James A.	Idaho										
McCormack, John W.	Massachusetts										
McCulloch, William M.	Ohio										
McDade, Joseph M.	Pennsylvania										
McDonald, Jack H.	Michigan										
McEwen, Robert C.	New York										
McFall, John J.	California										
McKneally, Martin B.	New York										
McMillan, John L.	South Carolina										
MacDonald, Torbert H.	Massachusetts										
MacGregor, Clark	Minnesota										
Madden, Ray J.	Indiana										
Mahon, George H.	Texas										
Mailliard, William S.	California										
Mann, James R.	South Carolina										
Marsh, John Ol, Jr.	Virginia										
Martin, Dave	Nebraska										
Mathias, Robert B.	California										
Matsunaga, Spark M.	Hawaii										
May, Catherine	Washington										
Mayne, Wiley	Iowa										
Meeds, Lloyd	Washington										

Melcher, John	Montana
Meskill, Thomas J.	Connecticut
Michel, Robert H.	Illinois
Mikva, Abner J.	Illinois
Miller, Clarence E.	Ohio
Miller, George P.	California
Mills, Wilbur D.	Arkansas
Minish, Joseph G.	New Jersey
Mink, Patsy	Hawaii
Minshall, William E.	Ohio
Mize, Chester L.	Kansas
Mizell, Wilmer	North Carolina
Mollohan, Robert H.	West Virginia
Monagan, John S.	Connecticut
Montgomery, G. V.	Mississippi
Moorhead, William S.	Pennsylvania
Morgan, Thomas E.	Pennsylvania
Morse, F. Bradford	Massachusetts
Morton, Rogers C. B.	Maryland
Mosher, Charles A.	Ohio
Moss, John E.	California
Murphy, John M.	New York
Murphy, William T.	Illinois
Myers, John T.	Indiana
Natcher, William H.	Kentucky
Nedzi, Lucien N.	Michigan

Nelsen, Ancher	Minnesota	☐	■	☐	☐	☐	☐	☐	☐	☐	☐	☐
Nichols, Bill	Alabama	▨	■	▨	☐	▨	▨	▨	▨	▨	▨	
Nix, Robert N. C.	Pennsylvania	■	☐	■	■	■	■	■	▨	■	■	■
Obey, David R.	Wisconsin	☐	■	■	☐	■	■	☐	☐	■	☐	
O'Hara, James G.	Michigan	▨	■	▨	☐	■	▨	■	▨	▨	▨	▨
O'Konski, Alvin E.	Wisconsin	■	☐	☐	☐	☐	☐	☐	☐	☐	☐	☐
Olsen, Arnold	Montana	☐	☐	☐	☐	☐	☐	☐	☐	☐	☐	☐
O'Neal, Maston	Georgia	▨	☐	☐	☐	☐	■	☐	☐	☐	☐	
O'Neill, Thomas P., Jr.	Massachusetts	■	☐	■	■	■	■	■	■	■	☐	
Ottinger, Richard L.	New York	☐	■	▨	■	■	■	▨	▨	▨	▨	
Passman, Otto E.	Louisiana	■	▨	■	■	▨	■	■	■	■	☐	■
Patman, Wright	Texas	■	☐	■	■	■	■	■	■	■	☐	
Patten, Edward J.	New Jersey	■	☐	■	☐	■	■	■	■	■	☐	
Pelly, Thomas M.	Washington	☐	▨	☐	☐	☐	☐	☐	☐	☐	☐	
Pepper, Claude	Florida	▨	☐	▨	☐	■	▨	▨	▨	▨	▨	
Perkins, Carl D.	Kentucky	☐	☐	☐	☐	▨	■	■	☐	☐	☐	
Pettis, Jerry L.	California	■	☐	■	☐	■	■	■	■	■	☐	
Philbin, Philip J.	Massachusetts	■	☐	▨	☐	■	■	■	■	■	■	
Pickley, J. J.	Texas	☐	☐	☐	☐	☐	☐	☐	☐	☐	☐	
Pike, Otis G.	New York	☐	■	▨	☐	▨	■	■	▨	▨	▨	
Pirnie, Alexander	New York	☐	☐	☐	☐	☐	☐	☐	☐	☐	☐	
Poage, W. R.	Texas	■	☐	☐	☐	▨	☐	■	▨	▨	■	
Podell, Bertram L.	New York	☐	☐	☐	☐	☐	☐	☐	☐	☐	☐	
Poff, Richard H.	Virginia	☐	☐	☐	☐	☐	☐	☐	☐	☐	☐	
Pollock, Howard W.	Alaska	▨	☐	▨	☐	☐	▨	▨	▨	▨	▨	☐
Powell, Adam C.	New York	▨				▨	▨	▨	■	▨	▨	

Preyer, Richardson	North Carolina										
Price, Melvin	Illinois	■	□	□	■	□	■	■	■	■	■
Price, Robert	Texas										
Pryor, David	Arkansas	□	□	□	■						
Pucinski, Roman C.	Illinois	□	□	□	■	▨	▨	▨	▨	▨	□
Purcell, Graham	Texas	□	□	□	■	▨	▨	▨	▨	▨	□
Quie, Albert H.	Minnesota	▨	□	□	■	▨	▨	▨	▨	▨	□
Quillen, James H. (Jimmy)	Tennessee	▨	□	□	■	□	□	□	□	□	□
Railsback, Tom	Illinois	▨	□	□	■	▨	□	□	□	▨	□
Randall, Wm. J.	Missouri	▨	□	□	■	□	□	□	□	□	□
Rarick, John R.	Louisiana	▨	□	□	■						
Rees, Thomas M.	California	▨	□	□	■	▨	▨	▨	▨	▨	□
Reid, Charlotte T.	Illinois	□	□	□	■	□	□	□	□	□	□
Reid, Ogden R.	New York	▨	□	□	■	▨	▨	▨	▨	▨	□
Reifel, Ben S.	South Dakota	□	□	□	■						
Reuss, Henry S.	Wisconsin	□	□	□	■	▨	▨	▨	▨	▨	□
Rhodes, John J.	Arizona	□	□	□	■					■	
Riegle, Donald W., Jr.	Michigan	▨	□	□	■	□	□	□	▨	▨	□
Rivers, L. Mendel	South Carolina	□	□	□	■	▨	▨	▨	■	■	□
Roberts, Ray	Texas	□	□	□	■	□	□	□	□	□	□
Robison, Howard W.	New York	□	□	□	■	□	□	□	□	□	□
Rodino, Peter W., Jr.	New Jersey	■	□	□	■	■	■	■	■	■	■
Roe, Robert A.	New Jersey	■	□	□	■	□	□	□	□	□	□
Rogers, Byron G.	Colorado	▨	□	■	■	□	□	□	□	□	□
Rogers, Paul G.	Florida	▨	□	□	■	□	□	□	□	□	□
Rooney, Fred B.	Pennsylvania										

Rooney, John J.	New York
Rosenthal, Benjamin S.	New York
Rostenkowski, Dan	Illinois
Roth, William V.	Delaware
Roudebush, Richard L.	Indiana
Roybal, Edward R.	California
Ruppe, Philip E.	Michigan
Ruth, Earl B.	North Carolina
Ryan, William F.	New York
St. Germain, Fernand J.	Rhode Island
Sandman, Charles W., Jr.	New Jersey
Satterfield, David E., III	Virginia
Saylor, John P.	Pennsylvania
Schadeberg, Henry C.	Wisconsin
Scherle, William J.	Iowa
Scheuer, James H.	New York
Schneebeli, Herman T.	Pennsylvania
Schwengel, Fred	Iowa
Scott, William Lloyd	Virginia
Sebelius, Keith G.	Kansas
Shipley, George	Illinois
Shriver, Garner E.	Kansas
Sikes, Robert L. F.	Florida
Sisk, B. F.	California
Skubitz, Joe	Kansas
Slack, John M.	West Virginia

Smith, H. Allen	California										
Smith, Henry P., III	New York										
Smith, Neal	Iowa										
Snyder, M. G. (Gene)	Kentucky										
Springer, William L.	Illinois										
Stafford, Robert T.	Vermont										
Staggers, Harley O.	West Virginia										
Stanton, J. William	Ohio										
Steed, Tom	Oklahoma										
Steiger, Sam	Arizona										
Steiger, William A.	Wisconsin										
Stephens, Robert G., Jr.	Georgia										
Stokes, Louis	Ohio										
Stratton, Samuel S.	New York										
Stubblefield, Frank A.	Kentucky										
Stuckey, W. S. (Bill), Jr.	Georgia										
Sullivan, Leonor K.	Missouri										
Symington, James W.	Missouri										
Taft, Robert, Jr.	Ohio										
Talcott, Burt L.	California										
Taylor, Roy A.	North Carolina										
Teague, Charles M.	California										
Teague, Olin E.	Texas										
Thompson, Fletcher	Georgia										
Thompson, Frank, Jr.	New Jersey										
Thomson, Vernon W.	Wisconsin										

Tiernan, Robert O.	Rhode Island											
Tunney, John V.	California											
Udall, Morris K.	Arizona											
Ullman, Al	Oregon											
Van Deerlin, Lionel	California											
Vander Jagt, Guy	Michigan											
Vanik, Charles A.	Ohio											
Vigorito, Joseph P.	Pennsylvania											
Waggonner, Joe D. Jr.	Louisiana											
Waldie, Jerome R.	California											
Wampler, William C.	Virginia											
Watson, Albert W.	South Carolina											
Watts, John C.	Kentucky											
Weicker, Lowell P., Jr.	Connecticut											
Whalen, Charles W., Jr.	Ohio											
Whalley, J. Irving	Pennsylvania											
White, Richard C.	Texas											
Whitehurst, G. William	Virginia											
Whitten, Jamie L.	Mississippi											
Widnall, William B.	New Jersey											
Wiggins, Charles E.	California											
Williams, Lawrence G.	Pennsylvania											
Wilson, Bob	California											
Wilson, Charles H.	California											
Winn, Larry, Jr.	Kansas											
Wold, John	Wyoming											

Wolff, Lester L.	New York										
Wright, Jim	Texas										
Wyatt, Wendell	Oregon										
Wydler, John W.	New York										
Wylie, Chalmers P.	Ohio										
Wyman, Louis C.	New Hampshire										
Yates, Sidney R.	Illinois										
Yatron, Gus	Pennsylvania										
Young, John	Texas										
Zablocki, Clement J.	Wisconsin										
Zion, Roger H.	Indiana										
Zwach, John M.	Minnesota										

(Ecology & War)

"....The need is not really for more brains, the need is now for **A GENTLER, A MORE TOLERANT PEOPLE THAN THOSE WHO WON FOR US AGAINST THE ICE, THE TIGER AND THE BEAR.** The hand that hefted the ax, out of some old blind allegiance to the past, fondles the machine gun as lovingly. It is a habit man will have to break to survive, but the roots go very deep." *(Loren Eiseley)*

This is the best statement we have seen relating ecology to the war and other social issues. It was to have been run as an ad in the *New York Times* and other major papers if money had been available.

Following this statement we are presenting the Society of Friends' analysis of voting records on these issues.

THIS ADVERTISEMENT is being placed by FRIENDS OF THE EARTH, a conservation group, but it concerns the war in Southeast Asia, and also wars in general.

Until recently conservationists have been thought of as content to fight the tragedy of a dam, the outrage of pollution, the spread of ugliness and environmental degradation, and also the economic and political solutions to that sort of mindless destruction.

Wars have been someone else's problem.

It has been as though war is not as destructive as dams. Or that an air pollution hazard in Los Angeles is a more significant danger to life than bombs landing upon non-combatants in a war, or the laterizing (turning to rock) of thousands of square miles of formerly living soil by widespread use of napalm. It is as though DDT in *our* vital tissues is worse than wartime chemical defoliants in the tissues of pregnant women.

It is not true. They are all of equal order, deriving as they do from a mentality which places all life and its vital sources in a position secondary to politics or power or profit.

Ecology teaches us that everything, *everything* is irrevocably connected. Whatever affects life in one place—*any* form of life, including people—affects other life elsewhere.

DDT on American farms, finds its way to Antarctic penguins.

Pollution in a trout stream eventually pollutes the ocean.

Smog over London blows over to Sweden.

An A-bomb explosion spreads radiation everywhere.

The movement of a dislodged, hungry, war torn population affects conditions and life wherever they go.

It is all connected. The doing of an act against life in one place is the doing of it everywhere. Thinking of things in any other way is like assuming it is possible to tear one stitch in a blanket without unraveling the blanket.

Friends of the Earth, therefore, its Board of Directors and staff, wishes to go on record in unanimous support of the recent telegram to Mr. Nixon, signed by the leaders of the nation's conservation organizations, reproduced below.

We would further like to urge readers of this ad to become involved in supporting the several resolutions now in the Congress which will hasten our withdrawal from Southeast Asia, as follows:

1) The Cooper-Church amendment which requires the withdrawal of all American military from Cambodia by June 30;

2) The Repeal of the Gulf of Tonkin resolution, used as the "legal" basis of the Vietnam involvement;

3) The McGovern-Hatfield Resolution, which requires total American disengagement by 1971.

Please write your congressmen and senators. In particular, write letters, or postcards or send wires to the list of senators who, at this time, have not gotten off the fence on this issue. [See coupon below for their names.] It is as significant an ecological act as blocking the SST, or turning in a car, or *not* buying a fur coat, or getting the lead out of gas. It is an act in favor of life.

Thank you.

FRIENDS OF THE EARTH
30 E. 42nd St., N.Y.C.—451 Pacific Ave., San Francisco
David Brower, President; Gary Soucie, Executive Director

On May 14, many of the nation's leading conservation figures joined in sending a telegram to Mr. Nixon. The telegram, and its signatories, are shown below. (Most signatories acted as individuals. Organizations are shown for identification).

"We call upon the administration, the Congress and the people of the United States to do whatever is necessary to bring about an immediate withdrawal of U.S. troops in Cambodia and a quick end to the war in Southeast Asia. There is no way in which the world can extricate itself from pressing problems of overpopulation and pollution without first halting the destructive drain on human and natural resources now demanded by the war. The time has come to recognize the war in Southeast Asia for what it really is—an ecological disaster that ultimately destroys both the land and the people it purports to protect.

The United States will survive neither as a political nation nor as an ecological unit if it persists in expanding its vital energy in irrelevant armed conflict. The great danger to the nation today lies not in our ideological or political differences but rather in our uncontrolled ability to destroy our common support system, the planet.

The war in Southeast Asia has legitimized total destruction as a strategy and is destroying the very ability of the land itself to support life in the future. The accepted policies of the war have included:
—The chemical defoliation of more than one-fifth of the forest area of South Vietnam—more than 5,000,000 acres. Beyond this disruption of life systems that promises to affect the future food supply of Vietnam, and the destruction of all other forms of life, this policy has accelerated rapid leaching of tropical soils and in some cases may cause permanent soil sterility.
—The systematic saturation bombing of entire land areas, square mile by square mile, to destroy all vegetation that might conceal or otherwise support the adversary.
—The destruction of entire crops—despite all evidence that military forces will *always* be fed first,

leaving children and the aged most likely to suffer.

"We believe that when an American commander can state (and believe) that 'We had to destroy the village to save it,' we face a danger to the earth of more immediacy than any other now being discussed.

"We believe that ecology, the study of the *interdependent* relationship of all things on earth, indicates the increasing penalty that will result from the needless destruction of life in any form. Our world has seemed so large for so long that horrible excesses in one place or another could be absorbed, and the earth counted upon to heal its wounds. But that is no longer true. The world is made smaller by our power, and the excesses are now so much greater.

"The natural balance is so delicate and complex that it seems to us that now is a time to encourage the diversity of life in all its forms and styles, and to replace the mentality that divides the world simplistically between 'us' and 'the enemy' with one that recognizes and celebrates diversity. We ask for a new, ecologically oriented foreign policy, one which places its emphasis on the needs of the ecosphere and not on the politics of nations. Such a policy may seem outrageous to those who consider conservation to be concerned only with strewn beer cans rather than strewn bodies, and with saving a recreation area rather than saving a planet. But a planet *is* at stake, and to save it we must begin by giving up the policy of destruction that leads with relentless logic to a My Lai —and to a widening of war in the interest of 'shortening' it.

"We cannot destroy Vietnam, or the world, in order to save it."

Donald Aitken, *Scientific coordinator, John Muir Institute;* Phillip Berry, *President, Sierra Club;* Raymond Balter, *Director, Ecology Center;* David Brower, *President, Friends of the Earth;* Harrison Brown, *California Institute of Technology;* David Challinor, *Smithsonian Institute;* Roland Clement, *Vice President, Audubon Society;* Eugene Coan, *Zero Population Growth;* Mrs. Kay Corbett, *Portland State*

University—*Environmental Teach-In Coordinator;* Garrett de Bell, *Editor, The Environmental Handbook;* Alvin Duskin; Dr. Paul Ehrlich, *President, Zero Population Growth;* Brock Evans, *Northwest Representative, Sierra Club;* Richard A. Falk, *Millbank Professor of International Law, Princeton University;* Francis Farquhar, *honorary President, Sierra Club;* Mrs. Francis Farquhar; Hans Feibush, *San Francisco Tomorrow;* David Forbes, *Grace Cathedral;* Harold Gilliam, *Conservation writer;* Garrett Hardin, *University of California, Santa Barbara;* Dennis Hayes, *National Coordinator, Earth Day;* Alfred Heller, *President, California Tomorrow;* Cliff Humphreys, *Ecology Action;* George Leonard, *author and editor;* A. Starker Leopold, *President, California Academy of Sciences;* Max Linn, *President, John Muir Institute;* Martin Litton, *Board of Directors, Friends of the Earth and Sierra Club;* Mark Lappe, *University of California, Berkeley;* Daniel Luten, *University of California, Berkeley;* Michael McCloskey, *Executive Director, Sierra Club;* Stephanie Mills, *Editor, Earth Times;* John Milton, *The Conservation Foundation;* Margaret Owings, *Save-the-Redwoods League;* Nathaniel Owings; Mr. and Mrs. George Plimpton; Eliot Porter, *photographer;* Douglas Scott, *The Wilderness Society;* Kevin Shea, *Science Editor, Environment;* Will Siri, *President, Save San Francisco Bay Association;* Gary Snyder, *Poet;* Dwight Steele, *Sierra Club;* John Fell Stevenson; Carl F. Stover, *Consultant, Washington, D.C.;* Stuart Udall, *Former Secretary of the Interior; President, Overview;* Richard A. Watson, *Washington University;* Kenneth Watt, *Institute of Ecology, University of California, Davis;* Robert Wenkham, *Friends of the Earth;* Thomas Whiteside; Willard Wirtz, *Former Secretary of Labor; Chairman of the Congress on Population and Environment;* Lawrence Williams, *Executive Director, Oregon Environmental Council;* Mrs. Maradel K. Gale, *President, Oregon Environmental Council;* Dr. Richard Gale, *Chairman Eugene group Pacific NW Chapter, Sierra Club;* Harvey Manning, *Editor, The Wild Cascade;* Dale Jones, *Editor, North*

West Conifer; Hon. Mrs. Maurine Neuberger, *Former United States Senator;* Dr. Donald McKinley, *Director, NW Environmental Defense Center;* William A. Nordstrom, *Wilderness photographer;* Mrs. Elizabeth Ducey, *Secretary, The Oregon Roadside Council;* Patrick D. Goldsworthy, *Former Director, Sierra Club.*

Mr. David Brower, FRIENDS OF THE EARTH
30 East 42nd Street, New York, N.Y. 10017

Dear Mr. Brower:

☐ I have sent letters urging support of anti-war bills to the following U.S. Senators who are as yet undecided on these measures.

☐ Sen. George Aitken   ☐ Sen. Jacob Javits
☐ Sen. Edward Brooke   ☐ Sen. Warren Magnuson
☐ Sen. Quentin Burdick   ☐ Sen. Joseph Montoya
☐ Sen. Clifford Case   ☐ Sen. Frank Moss
☐ Sen. Allen Ellender   ☐ Sen. Charles Percy
☐ Sen. Albert Gore   ☐ Sen. Stuart Symington

☐ I would like a copy of DEFOLIATION by Thomas Whiteside. I am enclosing one dollar. *(Includes tax.)*

☐ Please enroll me in your organization. I am enclosing $_____ for membership. ($15 regular, $5 spouse, $5 student, $25 supporting, $50 contributing, $250 life.)

☐ I would like to work on the war task force of Friends the Earth.

Name_____

Address_____

City_____ State_____ Zip_____

SOME KEY VOTES AND POSITIONS OF SENATORS AND REPRESENTATIVES

As evaluated by the Friends Committee on National Legislation of the American Friends Service Committee

Some Key Votes and Positions of Senators in 1969

1. Approval of resolution ratifying the **Nuclear Nonproliferation Treaty.** Ratified 83-15 (R 34-8; D 49-7) March 13.
2. Passage of the bill authorizing $480 million as the U.S. share of a $1.2 billion replenishment for the **International Development Association** (IDA.) Passed 49-34 (R 20-15; D 29-19) May 14.
3. Passage of resolution affirming the role of Congress in making **national commitments** (defined as use of U.S. armed forces on foreign territory or a promise to assist a foreign country by armed force or financial resources). Passed 70-16 (R 27-13; D 43-3) June 25.
4. Amendment by Sens. John Sherman Cooper, Ky. and Philip A. Hart, Mich. to **prohibit funds for deployment of Safeguard ABM system** but permit research and development. Rejected 49-51 (R 13-30; D 36-21) Aug. 6.
5. Amendment by Sen. Richard S. Schweiker, Pa., requiring regular **reports by the Defense Department on major contracts and for audits** and reports on such contracts by the General Accounting Office. Adopted 47-46 (R 18-22; D 29-24) Aug. 7.
6. Amendment by Sen. William Proxmire, Wis., **reducing funds for the Air Force C-54 trans-**

port plane procurement by $533 million and limiting to 58 the number that may be purchased until the Comptroller General made a study. Rejected 23-64 (R 6-33; D 17-31) Sept. 9.

7. Amendment by Sen. George McGovern, S.D., **authorizing free food stamps for families with monthly incomes under $60, authorizing $1.25 billion** for the program for fiscal 1970, and otherwise broadening existing law. Adopted 54-40 (R 16-27; D 38-13) Sept. 24.

8. Amendment by Sen. Peter H. Dominick to **cut $292.1 million from Office of Economic Opportunity programs** in fiscal year 1970. Adopted 47-38 (R 34-1; D 13-37) Oct. 14.

9. Amendment by Sen. George Murphy, Calif., giving **state Governors veto power over OEO legal services projects** and eliminating the OEO director's right to override the Governor's veto on legal services programs. Adopted 45-40 (R 30-6; D 15-34) Oct. 14.

10. Resolution expressing the sense of the Senate that the Administration **defer closing 59 Job Corps Centers** until Congress had reviewed anti-poverty legislation. Rejected 40-52 (R 0-40; D 40-12) May 13.

11. Senate Appropriations Committee amendment to **eliminate the House-passed $20,000 ceiling on agricultural subsidy payments** to individual farmers. Sen. John Williams, Del., charged that 13 farmers received payments of $500,000 to $1 million, and 5 received more than $1 million in subsidies. The $20,000 limitation was deleted 53-34 (R 25-13; D 28-21) July 7.

12. Motion by Sen. Thomas J. Dodd, Conn., to **prevent weakening of Gun Control Act of 1968.** The Finance Committee had added an amendment to the Interest Equalization Tax Act which repealed the requirement for keeping records of ammunition sales for rifles and shotguns. Sen.

Dodd's effort to delete the amendment was rejected 19-65 (R 7-28; D 12-37) Oct. 9.

13. Amendment by Sen. Stephen M. Young, Ohio, to **cut appropriations for Civil Defense Activities** to $64.2 million (an $8.3 million slash); rejected 19-49 (R 7-26; D 12-23) Nov. 11.

14. Sponsors of S. Res. 211 and others which urged the President to propose to the U.S.S.R. a **joint suspension of MIRV tests** (multiple nuclear warhead missiles). Sen. Edward W. Brooke, Mass., was chief sponsor of S. Res. 211 introduced June 17. 42 Senate sponsors.

■ = preferred by FCNL

☐ = unfavorable

▨ = absent

— = not in office

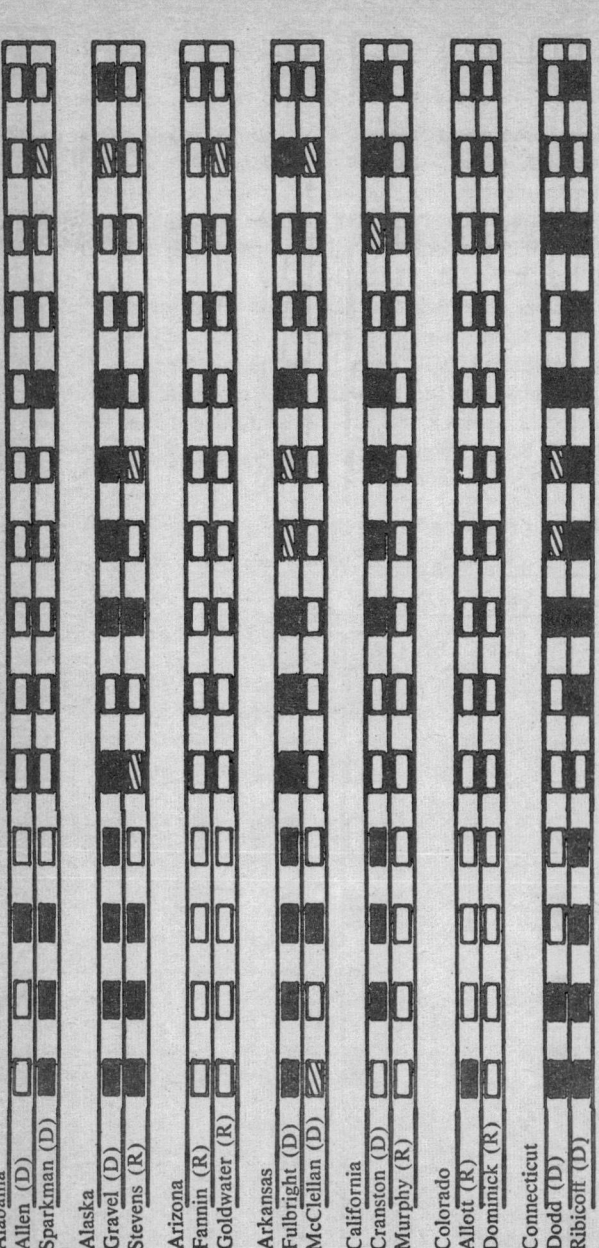

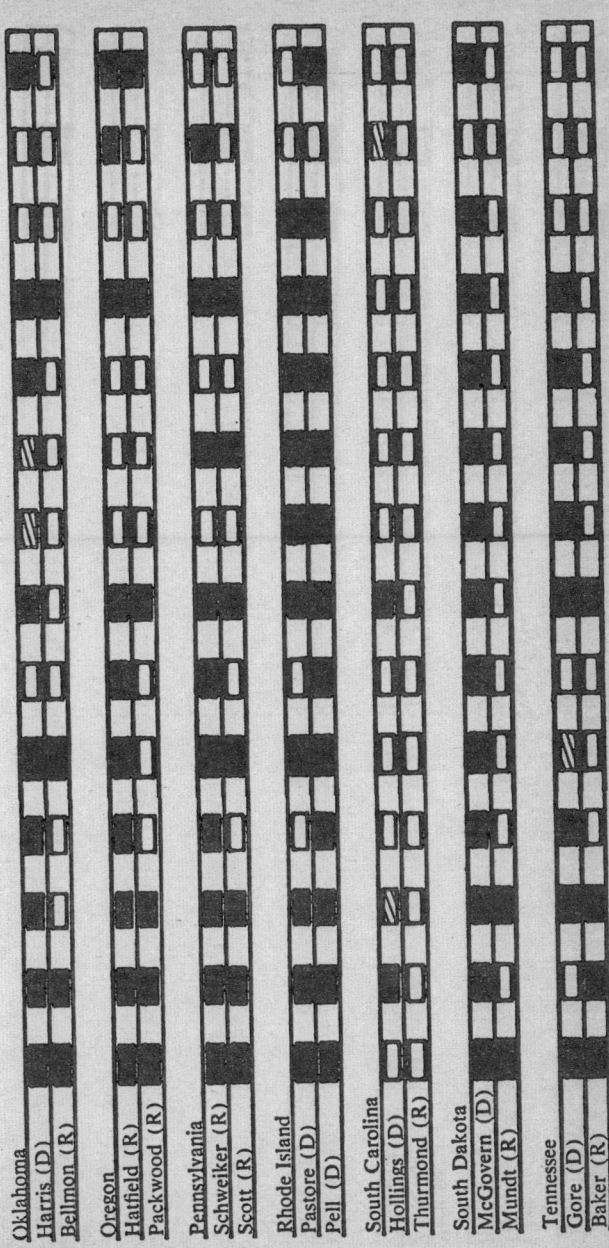

Texas
Yarborough (D)
Tower (R)

Utah
Moss (D)
Bennett (R)

Vermont
Aiken (R)
Prouty (R)

Virginia
Byrd, Jr. (D)
Spong (D)

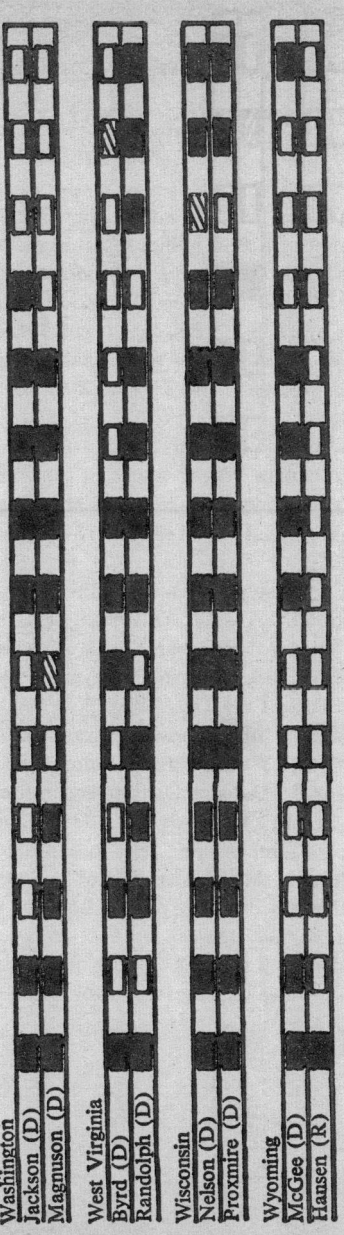

Some Key Votes and Positions of Representatives in 1969

1. Final passage of bill authorizing $480 million U.S. share of a $1.2 billion **replenishment for the International Development Association (IDA).** Passed 247-150 (R 85-94; D 162-56) March 12.
2. Motion by H. R. Gross, Ia., to **cut $11.1 million from the Peace Corps authorization** of $101.1 million. Rejected 144-186 (R 82-69; D 62-117) Sept. 8.
3. Motion to adjourn House and **terminate debate on the Vietnam War** at about 11 p.m. after only 2 of 20 scheduled speakers had been heard. Adjournment voted 112-110 (R 78-27; D 34-83) Oct. 14.
4. Motion to recommit Defense Procurement Authorization by Alvin E. O'Konski, Wis., to **delete $746.4 million for research and procurement of the Safeguard ABM system.** Rejected 93-270 (R 15-147; D 78-123) Oct. 3.
5. **Final passage of Defense Procurement Bill** authorizing $21.3 billion for procurement and research for the Defense Department in fiscal 1970. Passed 311-44 (R 154-5; D 157-39) Oct. 3.
6. Motion by John Young, Tex., to end debate and, in effect, **prevent consideration of major reforms in the military draft.** Approved 265-129 (R 147-26; D 118-103) Oct. 30.
7. Amendment by Charles S. Joelson, N.J., **adding $894,547,000 to appropriations for Office of Edu-**

cation programs. Approved 294-119 (R 99-81; D 195-38) July 31.

8. Amendment by Silvio O. Conte, Mass., **limiting farm subsidy payments to $20,000 for any one recipient.** Adopted 225-142 (R 107-53; D 118-89) May 27.

9. Motion by Donald G. Brotzman, Colo., to **recommit the Public Health Cigarette Smoking Act of 1969.** While the bill strengthened the warning label, it was generally regarded as a tobacco-industry and anti-government control bill since it prevented any restrictions on tobacco advertising for six years. Motion to recommit bill defeated 138-252 (R 52-124; D 86-128) June 18.

10. Motion by Charles W. Whalen, Jr., Ohio, to recommit military construction bill to **remove section preventing demonstrations and picketing at the Pentagon.** Defeated 87-323 (R 12-167; D 75-156) Aug. 5.

11. Motion by Ogden R. Reid, N.Y., to recommit resolution providing **$400,000 for investigative and other activities of the House Internal Security Committee.** Motion opposing funds defeated 73-284 (R 8-156; D 65-128) Apr. 1.

12. Sponsors of Vietnam War resolutions H. Con. Res. 403 (Oct. 9) and H. Res. 704 (Nov. 13) which call for **early and total withdrawal of all U.S. forces from Vietnam.** The list of 31 co-sponsors does not include all the House members who support this position, but it does indicate those members who are willing to take leadership in sponsoring resolutions.

13. Sponsors of H. Res. 613 (Nov. 4) and similar resolutions affirming "support of the President in his efforts to negotiate a just peace in Vietnam." This was an effort to **endorse the President's Vietnam policies** following his Nov. 3rd speech. 312 co-sponsors.

Alabama
3 Andrews (D)
7 Bevill (D)
5 Flowers (D)
8 Jones (D)
4 Nichols (D)
6 Buchanan (R)
2 Dickinson (R)
1 Edwards (R)

Alaska
AL Pollock (R)

Arizona
2 Udall (D)
1 Rhodes (R)
3 Steiger (R)

Arkansas
1 Alexander (D)
2 Mills (D)
4 Pryor (D)
3 Hammerschmidt (R)

California
5 Burton (D)
7 Cohelan (D)
9 Edwards (D)
34 Hanna (D)

2 Johnson (D)												
4 Leggett (D)												
15 McFall (D)												
8 Miller (D)												
3 Moss (D)												
16 Sisk (D)												
38 Tunney (D)												
37 Van Deerlin (D)												
14 Waldie (D)												
1 Clausen (R)												
10 Gubser (R)												
11 McCloskey (R)												
6 Mailliard (R)												
18 Mathias (R)												
33 Pettis (R)												
12 Talcott (R)												
13 Teague (R)												
35 Utt (R)												
36 Wilson (R)												
Los Angeles Co.												
17 Anderson (D)												
29 Brown (D)												
22 Corman (D)												
21 Hawkins (D)												
19 Holifield (D)												

26 Rees (D)													
30 Roybal (D)													
31 Wilson (D)													
28 Bell (R)													
23 Clawson (R)													
32 Hosmer (R)													
24 Lipscomb (R)													
27 Goldwater (R)													
20 Smith (R)													
25 Wiggins (R)													

Colorado

4 Aspinall (D)													
3 Evans (D)													
1 Rogers (D)													
2 Brotzman (R)													

Connecticut

1 Daddario (D)													
3 Giaimo (D)													
5 Monagan (D)													
2 St. Onge (D)													
6 Meskill (R)													
4 Weicker (R)													

Delaware

AL Roth (R)													

Florida

3 Bennett (D)												
4 Chappell (D)												
12 Fascell (D)												
2 Fuqua (D)												
6 Gibbons (D)												
7 Haley (D)												
11 Pepper (D)												
9 Rogers (D)												
1 Sikes (D)												
10 Burke (R)												
8 Cramer (R)												
5 Frey (R)												

Georgia

3 Brinkley (D)												
7 Davis (D)												
6 Flynt (D)												
1 Hagan (D)												
9 Landrum (D)												
2 O'Neal (D)												
10 Stephens (D)												
8 Stuckey (D)												
4 Blackburn (R)												
5 Thompson (R)												

Hawaii
AL Matsunaga (D)
AL Mink (D)

Idaho
2 Hansen, O. (R)
1 McClure (R)

Illinois
21 Gray (D)
24 Price (D)
23 Shipley (D)
16 Anderson (R)
17 Arends (R)
14 Erlenborn (R)
20 Findley (R)
12 McClory (R)
18 Michel (R)
19 Railsback (R)
15 Reid (R)
22 Springer (R)

Chicago-Cook Co.
7 Annunzio (D)
1 Dawson (D)
5 Kluczynski (D)
2 Mikva (D)

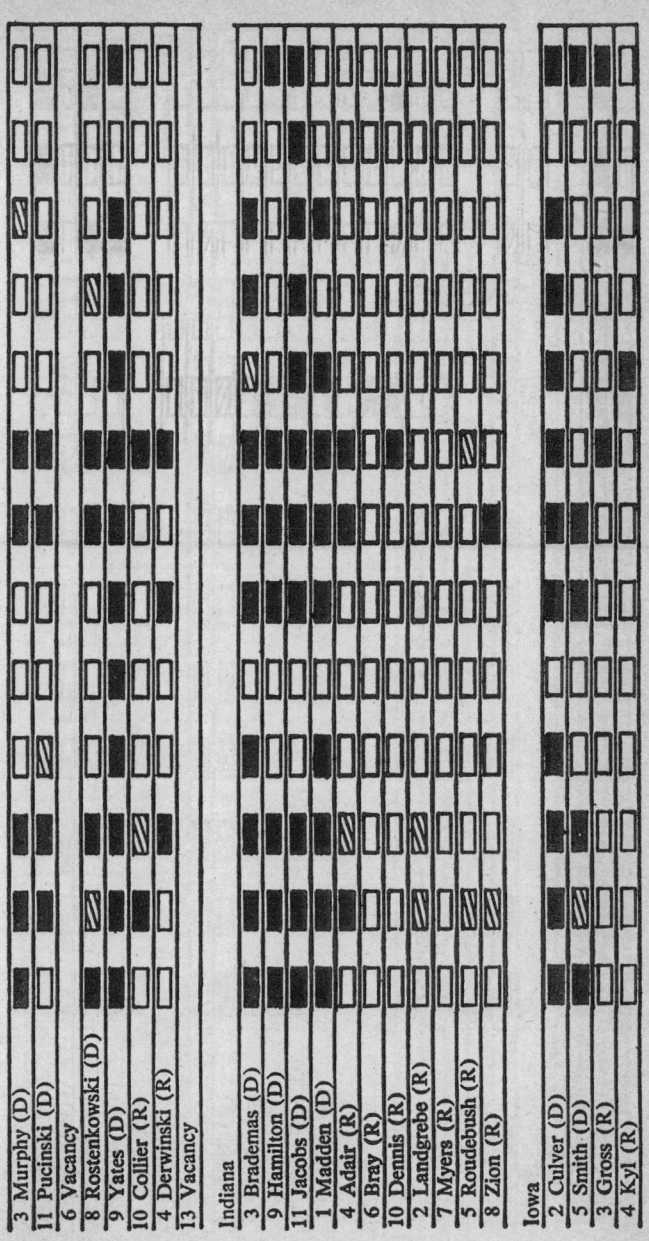

6 Mayne (R)
7 Scherle (R)
1 Schwengel (R)

Kansas
2 Mize (R)
1 Sebelius (R)
4 Shriver (R)
5 Skubitz (R)
3 Winn (R)

Kentucky
2 Natcher (D)
7 Perkins (D)
1 Stubblefield (D)
6 Watts (D)
5 Carter (R)
3 Cowger (R)
4 Snyder (R)

Louisiana
2 Boggs (D)
3 Caffery (D)
7 Edwards (D)
1 Herbert (D)
8 Long (D)
5 Passman (D)

Representative												
6 Rarick (D)	☐	☐	☒	☐	☐	☐	☐	☐	☐	☐	■	☐
4 Waggonner (D)	☐	☐	☒	☐	☐	☐	☐	☐	☐	☐	■	☐
Maine												
2 Hathaway (D)	■	☐	☒	■	☐	☐	■	☐	■	☐	■	■
1 Kyros (D)	■	■	☒	■	☐	☐	■	☐	■	☐	■	■
Maryland												
4 Fallon (D)	■	☒	☒	☐	☐	■	■	☐	☐	☐	☒	☐
4 Friedel (D)	■	☐	■	☐	☐	■	■	☐	☐	☐	☐	☐
3 Garmatz (D)	■	☒	■	☐	☐	■	■	☐	☐	☐	☒	☐
2 Long (D)	■	☐	☐	☐	☐	■	■	☐	☐	☐	☐	☐
6 Beall (R)	■	☐	☐	☐	☐	■	■	☐	☐	☐	☐	☐
8 Gude (R)	■	☐	☐	☐	☐	■	■	☐	☐	☐	☒	☐
5 Hogan (R)	■	☐	☐	☐	☐	☐	☐	☐	☐	☐	☐	☐
1 Morton (R)	■	☐	☐	☐	☐	■	☐	☐	☐	☐	☐	☐
Massachusetts												
2 Boland (D)	■	■	☐	■	☐	☐	■	☐	■	☐	■	■
11 Burke (D)	■	■	☒	■	☐	☐	■	☐	■	☐	■	■
4 Donohue (D)	■	■	☒	■	☐	☐	■	☐	■	☐	■	■
6 Harrington (D)	■	─	─	■	─	─	■	─	■	─	■	■
7 Macdonald (D)	■	■	☒	■	☐	☐	■	☐	■	☐	■	■
9 McCormack (D)	─	─	─	─	─	─	─	─	─	─	─	─
8 O'Neill (D)	■	■	☐	■	☐	☐	■	☐	■	☐	■	■
3 Philbin (D)	■	■	☐	■	☐	☐	■	☐	■	☐	■	■
1 Conte (R)	■	■	☒	■	☐	☐	■	☐	■	☐	■	■

10 Heckler (R)	■	□	□	■	■	■	■	□	■	■	■	■	■
12 Keith (R)	□	□	□	■	□	■	■	□	■	⊘	■	■	■
5 Morse (R)	□	□	□	■	□	■	■	□	■	■	■	■	■

Michigan

12 O'Hara (D)	□	□	□	□	⊘	□	■	□	□	□	■	■	■
18 Broomfield (R)	□	□	□	□	□	■	■	□	■	■	■	■	■
3 Brown (R)	□	□	□	□	□	■	■	□	■	⊘	■	■	■
10 Cederberg (R)	□	□	⊘	□	□	■	■	□	■	⊘	■	⊘	■
6 Chamberlain (R)	□	□	□	□	□	■	⊘	□	■	■	■	■	■
2 Esch (R)	□	□	⊘	□	□	□	■	□	⊘	■	■	■	■
5 Ford (R)	□	□	□	□	□	□	⊘	□	⊘	■	⊘	⊘	■
8 Harvey (R)	□	□	⊘	□	□	■	■	□	■	■	■	■	■
4 Hutchinson (R)	□	□	□	■	□	■	■	□	■	⊘	■	■	■
19 McDonald (R)	□	□	□	□	□	■	■	□	■	■	■	■	■
7 Riegle (R)	□	□	□	□	□	■	■	□	⊘	⊘	⊘	□	■
11 Ruppe (R)	□	□	□	■	□	□	□	□	□	■	⊘	□	■
9 Vander Jagt (R)	□	□	□	□	□	■	■	□	■	■	■	■	■

Detroit-Wayne Co.

1 Conyers (D)	■	□	□	□	⊘	■	■	□	■	⊘	■	■	■
13 Diggs (D)	■	□	□	□	□	■	■	□	■	⊘	■	■	■
16 Dingell (D)	■	□	□	□	□	■	■	□	■	■	■	■	■
15 Ford (D)	■	□	□	□	□	■	■	□	■	⊘	■	■	■
17 Griffiths (D)	■	□	□	□	□	■	■	□	■	⊘	⊘	■	■
14 Nedzi (D)	■	□	□	□	□	■	■	□	■	⊘	■	■	■

Minnesota

- 8 Blatnik (D)
- 5 Fraser (D)
- 4 Karth (D)
- 7 Langen (R)
- 3 MacGregor (R)
- 2 Nelsen (R)
- 1 Quie (R)
- 6 Zwach (R)

Mississippi

- 1 Abernethy (D)
- 5 Colmer (D)
- 3 Griffin (D)
- 4 Montgomery (D)
- 2 Whitten (D)

Missouri

- 5 Bolling (D)
- 10 Burlison (D)
- 1 Clay (D)
- 6 Hull (D)
- 9 Hungate (D)
- 8 Ichord (D)
- 4 Randall (D)
- 3 Sullivan (D)

Representative													
2 Symington (D)	■	□	■	□	□	■	■	□	□	□	□	□	■
7 Hall (R)	□	■	□	□	□	□	□	□	□	□	□	□	□
Montana													
2 Melcher (D)	■	▨	□	□	□	□	■	–	–	□	□	□	□
1 Olsen (D)	■	■	□	□	□	□	□	▨	–	□	□	□	□
Nebraska													
2 Cunningham (R)	▨	□	▨	□	□	▨	□	□	□	□	□	□	□
1 Denney (R)	□	□	▨	□	□	□	■	□	□	□	□	□	□
3 Martin (R)	□	■	▨	□	□	□	■	▨	□	□	□	□	□
Nevada													
AL Baring (D)	□	□	□	□	□	▨	□	□	▨	□	□	□	□
New Hampshire													
2 Cleveland (R)	□	□	■	□	□	□	□	□	■	□	□	□	□
1 Wyman (R)	□	□	□	□	□	□	□	□	□	□	□	□	□
New Jersey													
14 Daniels (D)	■	■	■	□	□	■	■	□	■	□	■	□	□
13 Gallagher (D)	□	▨	■	▨	□	■	▨	□	□	□	■	■	□
9 Helstoski (D)	■	■	■	□	□	■	■	▨	□	□	■	■	■
3 Howard (D)	▨	■	■	□	□	■	■	□	□	■	■	□	■
8 Vacancy													
11 Minish (D)	■	■	■	□	□	■	■	□	□	□	■	□	□
15 Patten (D)	■	■	■	□	□	■	■	□	□	□	■	□	■
10 Rodino (D)	▨	■	■	□	□	■	■	□	□	□	■	□	□

4 Thompson (D)														
6 Cahill (R)														
12 Dwyer (R)														
5 Frelinghuysen (R)														
1 Hunt (R)														
2 Sandman (R)														
7 Widnall (R)														

New Mexico

2 Foreman (R)														
1 Lujan (R)														

New York

41 Dulski (D)														
34 Hanley (D)														
5 Lowenstein (D)														
39 McCarthy (D)														
25 Ottinger (D)														
1 Pike (D)														
35 Stratton (D)														
3 Wolff (D)														
29 Button (R)														
37 Conable (R)														
28 Fish (R)														
2 Grover (R)														
38 Hastings (R)														
36 Horton (R)														

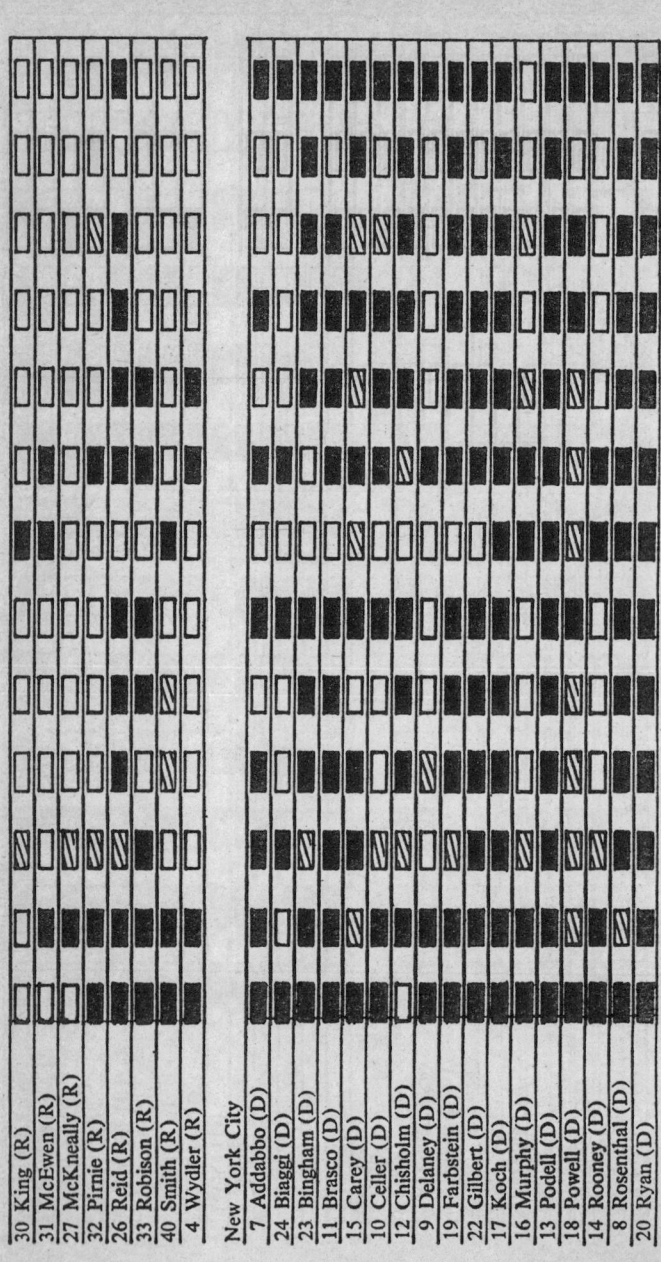

21 Scheuer (D)												
6 Halpern (R)												

North Carolina

2 Fountain (D)												
4 Galifianakis (D)												
3 Henderson (D)												
1 Jones (D)												
7 Lennon (D)												
6 Preyer (D)												
11 Taylor (D)												
10 Broyhill (R)												
9 Jonas (R)												
5 Mizell (R)												
8 Ruth (R)												

North Dakota

1 Andrews (R)												
2 Kleppe (R)												

Ohio

9 Ashley (D)												
20 Feighan (D)												
18 Hays (D)												
19												
21 Stokes (D)												
22 Vanik (D)												
17 Ashbrook (R)												
14 Ayres (R)												

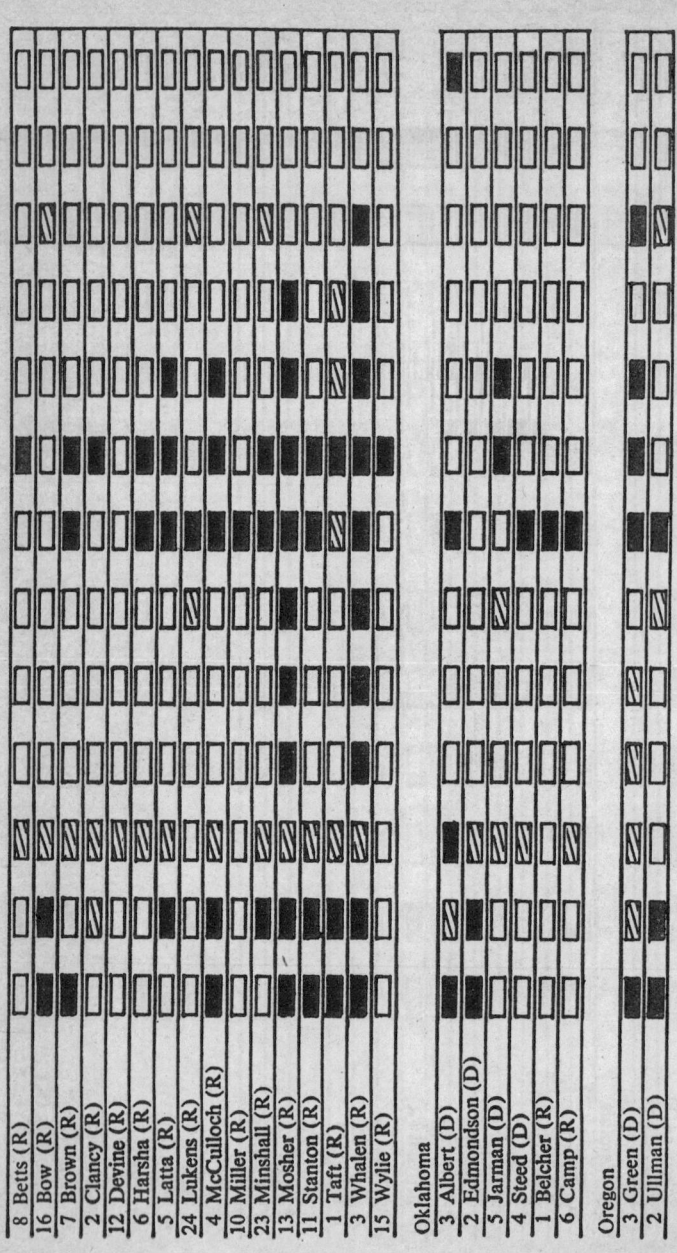

4 Dellenback (R)	■	■			■	■						
1 Wyatt (R)	■	□			■	■	⊠					
Pennsylvania												
25 Clarke (D)		□	⊠	⊠	■	■	⊠					
21 Dent (D)		■	□	□	■	■						
11 Flood (D)		■	⊠	□	■	■	□					
20 Gaydos (D)		■	■	□	■	■			■			
14 Moorhead (D)	□	■	□	□	■	■						
26 Morgan (D)		■	⊠	⊠	■	■						
15 Rooney (D)		■	⊠	⊠	■	■						
24 Vigorito (D)		■	■	⊠	■	■						
6 Yatron (D)					■	■						
8 Biester (R)		■			■	■						
18 Corbett (R)		■		⊠	■	■						
13 Coughlin (R)					■	■						
16 Eshleman (R)		⊠			■	■						
27 Fulton (R)					■	■						
19 Goodling (R)					■	□						
23 Johnson (R)		■			■	□						
10 McDade (R)					■	■			■			
22 Saylor (R)		□		⊠	■	■						
17 Schneebeli (R)		⊠	■		■	□						
9												
12 Whalley (R)	⊠	⊠			■	■	⊠					
7 Williams (R)		□			■	□						

Philadelphia City
1 Barrett (D)
3 Byrne (D)
4 Eilberg (D)
5 Green (D)
2 Nix (D)

Rhode Island
1 St. Germain (D)
2 Tiernan (D)

South Carolina
3 Dorn (D)
5 Gettys (D)
6 McMillan (D)
4 Mann (D)
1 Rivers (D)
2 Watson (R)

South Dakota
2 Berry (R)
1 Reifel (R)

Tennessee
6 Anderson (D)
7 Blanton (D)
4 Evins (D)
5 Fulton (D)

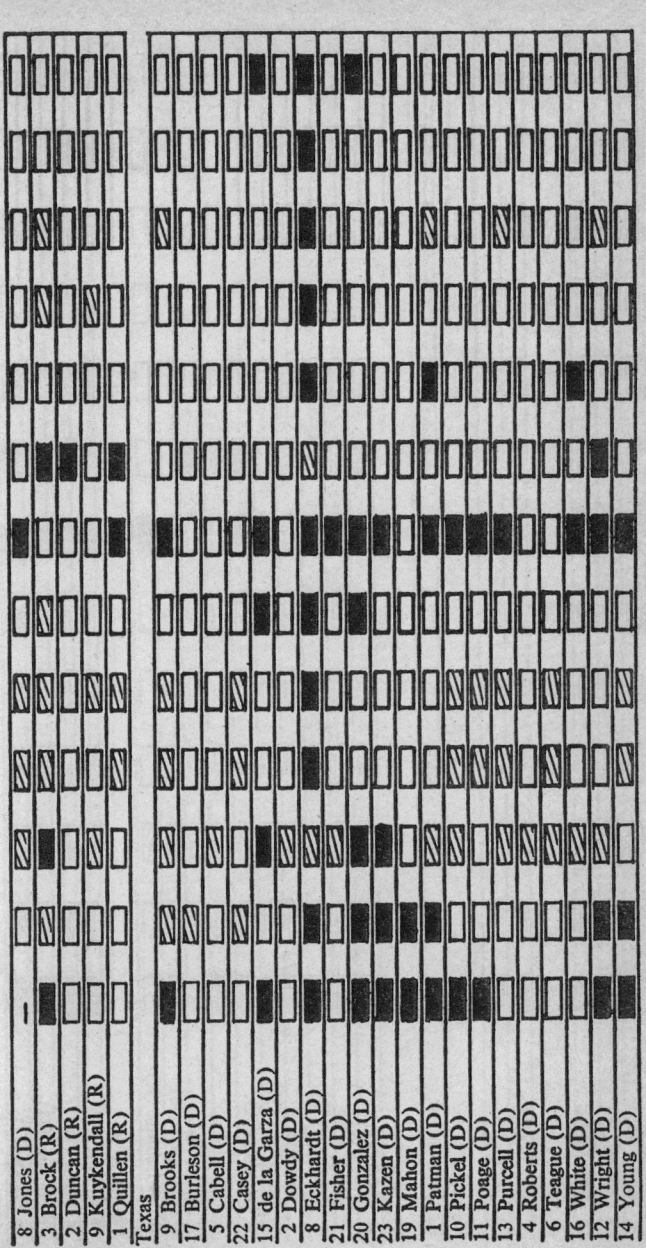

Representative															
7 Bush (R)															
3 Collins (R)															
18 Price (R)															

Utah

1 Burton (R)															
2 Lloyd (R)															

Vermont

AL Stafford (R)															

Virginia

4 Abbitt (D)															
5 Daniel (D)															
1 Downing (D)															
7 Marsh (D)															
3 Satterfield (D)															
10 Broyhill (R)															
6 Poff (R)															
8 Scott (R)															
9 Wampler (R)															
2 Whitehurst (R)															

Washington

7 Adams (D)															
5 Foley (D)															
3 Hansen (D)															
6 Hicks (D)															

West Virginia
- 2 Meeds (D)
- 4 May (R)
- 1 Pelley (R)

West Virginia
- 4 Hechler (D)
- 5 Kee (D)
- 1 Mollohan (D)
- 3 Slack (D)
- 2 Staggers (D)

Wisconsin
- 2 Kastenmeier (D)
- 7 Obey (D)
- 5 Reuss (D)
- 4 Zablocki (D)
- 8 Byrnes (R)
- 9 Davis (R)
- 10 O'Konski (R)
- 1 Schadeberg (R)
- 6 Steiger (R)
- 3 Thomson (R)

Wyoming
- AL Wold (R)

Contributors

GEORGE ALDERSON has a B.A. in Biology from Reed College and did graduate work in range management at Utah State University. He is legislative director of Friends of the Earth in Washington, D. C. During his five years as a conservation leader in Washington he participated in many environmental campaigns including assisting the Sierra Club as a volunteer in lobbying to defeat the Grand Canyon dams.

DAVID BROWER is president of Friends of the Earth, director of the John Muir Institute for Environmental Studies, and founder of the League of Conservation Voters. He served for 17 years as executive director of the Sierra Club and was a founder of Trustees for Conservation, the North Cascades Conservation Council, and the Sierra Club Foundation. He was general editor of the first twenty volumes of the club's Exhibit Format Series and is now serving that function for the FOE international series of exhibit books, *The Earth's Wild Places*.

GARRETT DE BELL has a B.A. in Biology from Stanford University and was a Ph.D. candidate in ecology (zoology) at the University of California, Berkeley. He edited *The Environmental Handbook* and was a Washington lobbyist for Zero Population Growth.

CLAYTON DENMAN is an associate professor at Central Washington State College and President of the Small Towns Institute. He received the Ph.D. in anthropology from the University of California at Berkeley and now lives in the small town of Ellensburg, Washington. He has studied several mining and agricultural towns and a small town on an Indian reservation.

CONTRIBUTORS

JOHN C. ESPOSITO is a member of the Washington, D. C. bar who has studied regulatory and business matters for three years. He is a staff consultant to Ralph Nader's Center for Study of Responsive Law and counsel to Environmental Action, Washington, D. C. He edited a "Nader's Raiders" task force report on air pollution which has recently been published by Grossman Publishers, New York, under the title *Vanishing Air*.

ROBERT FELLMETH graduated from Harvard Law School in 1970 and is working as an aide to Ralph Nader. One of the original "Nader's Raiders," he has co-authored two books on government agencies: *The Nader Report on the Federal Trade Commission*, and *The Interstate Commerce Omission*.

JOAN MCINTYRE is studying to be an Earth Housekeeper, lives with two Siberian Huskies, and is the founding organizer of the Ladies Lunar League (membership open).

HARVEY MANNING is the editor of *The Wild Cascades*.

RICHARD H. MEEKER is a recent graduate of Amherst College. He is presently a schoolteacher in Ocracoke, North Carolina.

BRENN STILLEY is a free-lance environmental writer, whose work has appeared in the *Earth Times*, San Francisco *Chronicle* Sunday magazine section, and *The Environmental Handbook*, among other publications.

THOMAS M. TURNER received a B.A. in Political Science from the University of California, Berkeley. After two years in the Peace Corps in Turkey, and a year with the Sierra Club, he joined David Brower at Friends of the Earth.

HARRISON WELLFORD works with Ralph Nader in Washington, D. C. and for the past year has been Executive Director of the Center for the Study of Responsive Law (the home of Nader's Raiders). He has a master's degree from Cambridge University and is a Ph.D. candidate in government at Harvard University, and is the author of the forthcoming book *Sowing the Wind,* a study of the Department of Agriculture stressing federal pesticide policy and federal rural poverty programs.

REPRESENTATIVE MORRIS K. UDALL, Democrat from Arizona, combines a long term interest in Congressional reform with a long term interest in the environment. He has played a key role in many conservation fights in Congress.

REPRESENTATIVE PAUL N. MCCLOSKEY, Republican of San Mateo County, California, is a leading advocate of sound environmental policy in the House of Representatives. He serves on the Conservation and Natural Resources Subcommittee and the Merchant Marine and Fisheries Committees, as well as on the Republican task force on earth resources and population. He was Co-Chairman, with Senator Gaylord Nelson, of Earth Day (the Environmental Teach-In). He is a strong spokesman for Congressional reform and effective environmental legislation.

APPENDIX

What a Survival Library Can Do for You

A STATEMENT BY THE PUBLISHERS

The purpose of the Ballantine/Friends of the Earth Survival Series is to provide the best possible information, written for the intelligent layman, about the principal current threats to the environment that urgently demand remedial action.

We hope to encourage support for the further research that will always be necessary as long as man uses technology and seeks to anticipate the consequences. Proper application of science and humanity will sometimes show that man had better not do what mere technology tells him he can do.

We will also urge action now, based upon what is already known, to prevent using a given technology in advance of assurance that it will not inflict lasting harm.

The "What You Can Do" department of the series is important, but the book is the thing. Each book is intended to fill what has been a gap in publishing. Ordinarily, books take too much lead time to be of current value. We have sped them up so that vital information—the abstract (the contents page and the promotional material), the detailed exposition (the text itself, with such illustrations as there are available), and the documentation—can become a readily available part of the concerned citizen's working library. Many magazines require more lead time than these books do, and those that are published on a news-magazine schedule rarely have enough space to provide all the material you may need at hand. And in all but the best organized of homes, magazines have a way of being topped by succeeding issues so rapidly that the lode-bearing strata are lost to all time and to the *Reader's Guide to Periodical Literature*—which is not in many home reference libraries.

We should like to think, further, that the series will be reviewed, interpreted, and enlarged upon in the very media whose limitations we have remarked upon, and nevertheless valued very highly for their own unique and indispensable role in letting people know enough about what is happening to their environment in time to save it.

So here is retrievable information for you to put to good use.

—IAN BALLANTINE, *President*
Ballantine Books

—DAVID BROWER, *President*
Friends of the Earth

What You Can Do

ORGANIZATIONS YOU MAY WISH TO SUPPORT

By placing emphasis in the following pages on the organizations that are not tax-deductible and thus are handicapped in fund-seeking we do not wish to derogate the others. They are indispensable, as is the team, no matter how the present tax laws separate them.

In the diversity of conservation organizations is their strength. The composite of varying purposes, leadership, following, and sources of financial support is what gives the conservation movement its force.

The combined annual budgets of all the conservation organizations, deductible and nondeductible would run the Pentagon's effort for about four hours.

To alleviate the environmental crisis, here is what three new organizations are doing in behalf of the preservation, restoration, and rational use of the ecosphere.

The John Muir Institute for Environmental Studies, founded in New Mexico in 1968, is tax-deductible. It assumes that the conservationist's cause is good and his heart in the right place, but that he deserves better information. The Institute seeks membership support for its conferences, research, and publishing program.

Friends of the Earth, founded in New York in 1969, rejoins that the researcher's cause is good, but that unless we act now on what he already knows or reasonably suspects, he may never complete his studies. FOE is not tax–deductible because it lobbies substantially.

The League of Conservation Voters began operation in Washington, D.C. in March 1970 to make sure that environmental issues receive the attention they should, before, during, and after U.S. elections. It intends to help put and keep in office men and women who support the broad Muir & Friends goals.

Complementing each other, but separate to meet the requirements of law, the trio can help existing conservation organizations get new things accomplished. John Muir had all these things in mind a century ago, shortly after he arrived from Scotland. Looking upon the natural beauty he found, he wrote, "The grand show is eternal." We would keep it that way, our view of man's primary responsibility to man.

THE JOHN MUIR INSTITUTE (JMI) conducts three concurrent educational, scientific, and literary undertakings:

Conferences: Under the series title, "Forum for a Future", JMI has held two conferences at Aspen, Colorado. The first, "Progress in a Living Environment," held in 1969, brought together participants from many fields and age groups, from Watts to the White House, to explore routes to a dynamic equilibrium between man and the environment. The second, held in 1970, titled "Is Survival Economically Feasible?" again brought together people from many fields—many of them economists, one an urban sociologist from London—to explore the ground for a major conference in 1971, "Making Survival Economically Attractive." Four books deriving from these conferences are in preparation; still others are likely to appear. Other conferences being organized relate to an ecological view of water development, advertising for (or versus?) the environment, and keeping the ecosphere insurable.

ORGANIZATIONS YOU MAY WISH TO SUPPORT

John Muir Institute is undertaking to fill in gaps on the research map by 1) independent analysis and 2) critique of major environment–disrupting projects, 3) inquiry into the forces and rates of environmental restoration, 4) certification of fair–conservation practices, and 5) development of ecological conscience in all professions.

Wherever possible, JMI will seek to encourage the carrying out of such research in existing facilities; it has a working agreement, for example, with the University of New Mexico. Current projects include: presentation of an independent analysis of the California Water Plan, a critique of the Glen Canyon project, an inquiry into tundra recovery, and completion of a manuscript on ecological conscience in teaching.

Publishing: JMI arranges for the preparation of illustrated, edited manuscripts for publication, including the international exhibit series, The Earth's Wild Places, portraying the beauty, diversity, and organic wholeness of life and the natural environment of the planet.

The series recognizes, as Muir did, that wilderness holds answers to questions man has not yet learned how to ask. Through blending of photographs, prose, and poetry, each book reflects a particular environment and the local culture's view of its relation to man. Each volume is to appear first in exhibit size for U.S. and European use and later in an inexpensive paperback edition. More than one hundred volumes are envisioned over the next two decades.

John Muir Institute Board of Directors: ROBERT O. ANDERSON, Roswell, New Mexico, *Chairman of the Board;* MAX LINN, Albuquerque, *President;* DAVID R. BROWER, Berkeley, *Vice–President and Director;* DAVID SIVE, New York, *Secretary;* IBEN BROWNING, Palo Alto; DONALD W. AITKEN, Woodside, California, *Scientific Coordinator.*

FRIENDS OF THE EARTH (FOE)

Legislative action: Friends of the Earth has four registered lobbyists in Washington. Zero Population Growth also has four, Environmental Action has three, Trustees for Conservation and Citizens Committee on Natural Resources have one each, giving the conservation lobby a total of 13. FOE expends a major part of its funds in advocating good environmental legislation as part of a team. Major projects have been opposition to the SST, moving the proposed jetport safely away from the Everglades, assuring a water supply for the Everglades, opposing the Cross–Florida Barge Canal, and constant assistance and frequent testimony on the Hill.

Legal action; rallying public support: FOE joined with The Wilderness Society and Environmental Defense Fund in obtaining an injunction against the Trans–Alaska Pipeline. It has filed a formal complaint with the FCC seeking an equal audience under the Fairness Doctrine for arguments countering the anti–environmental advertising by the automobile and oil industries that portray as clean the major contributors to air pollution, as recognized by the Nixon Administration and others. FOE is helping to protect South Carolina from the proposed BASF chemical plant and port; the Pacific Coast from the California Water Plan; and furbearing animals from wearers of wild fur in an effective campaign in the market place based on the theme, "Furs look better on their original owners".

International: Many conservation problems abroad start in the U.S., where 6 per cent of the earth's population is using more than half the earth's resources and seeking to increase its share. FOE organizations abroad are also needed. *Les Amis de la Terre* has started in France, and two books by French authors are in process. FOE's representative in Switzerland is undertaking preparatory work in other countries. For FOE's primary international effort, see below.

Publishing: Where JMI's work ends in the publishing operation, FOE's begins, with McCall Publishing Company and others, as appropriate. Among the titles scheduled in "The Earth's Wild Places" series are:

ORGANIZATIONS YOU MAY WISH TO SUPPORT

Maui: The Last Hawaiian Place, Robert Wenkam and Kenneth Brower
Return to the Alps, Max Knight and Gerhard Klammet
Point Lobos and Its Oceans, Richard Kauffman and John Hay
Brooks Range: Rivers of Stone, Seas of Grass, K. Brower, introd., John Milton
"It's only a little planet . . .", John Milton and Noel Simon, introd., F. Fraser Darling
A Sense of Place, Alan Gussow
Mekong River, Sterling Seagrave and John Milton
Hokkaido: Wilderness in Japan, Gary Snyder and Franz Berko
Micronesia: Pacific Wilderness, Robert Wenkam and Kenneth Brower
The Highlands and the Marks of Renewal, W. H. Murray and Wayne Sourbeer
Rocky Mountain Trench: No Place to Flood, Martin Litton
Golden Islands: Georgia's Wild Coast, James Valentine and Robert Hanie

In smaller format:
Fragile Craft, David Brower

FOE/Ballantine Books (paperback) Already Published:

The S/S/T and Sonic Boom Handbook, William A. Shurcliff
The Environmental Handbook, Garrett De Bell, ed.
Defoliation, Thomas Whiteside; foreword, George Wald

In press:

The Nuclear Dilemma, Gene Bryerton, foreword by David R. Inglis
The Users' Guide to the Protection of the Environment, Paul Swatek

The Householder's Environmental Guide, Paul Swatek
The Forest for the Trees, Harmon Henkin
The Environmental Handbook: II, Garrett De Bell, ed.
Teaching for Survival, Mark Terry

FOE/other publishers:

Seventeen other titles are under active consideration, plus calendars, posters, and notes.

Task forces

Specific FOE task forces are set up to fight particular battles; to be phased out when the battles end. Conservation advertisements will help them, as will the solutions-for-survival library made possible by the publishing program.

The acronym FOE troubles some people briefly, but the suggested paradox is appropriate: friends of the earth must be foe of forces degrading the earth.

Leadership

Friends of the Earth Board of Directors: DAVID R. BROWER, Berkeley, *President;* STEWART M. OGILVY, Yonkers, and MAX LINN, Albuquerque, *Vice-Presidents;* DAVID SIVE, New York, *Member executive committee;* ALFRED S. FORSYTH, New York, *Treasurer;* PERRY H. KNOWLTON, New York, *Secretary;* DONALD W. AITKEN, Woodside, California; LUNA B. LEOPOLD, Washington, D.C.; DANIEL B. LUTEN, Berkeley; JERRY MANDER, San Francisco; EDWIN S. MATTHEWS, Paris; JOHN P. MILTON, Washington, D.C.; GARY A. SOUCIE, New York; ROBERT STEIN, New York.

Friends of the Earth Advisory Council: HARRISON BROWN, CHARLES CALLISON, BARRY COMMONER, NORMAN COUSINS, PAUL EHRLICH, DUKE ELLINGTON, ARTHUR GODFREY, ARLO GUTHRIE, HENRY MAKOWSKI, STEPHANIE MILLS, GEORGE PLIMPTON, ELIOT PORTER, PETE SEEGER,

Noel Simon, C. P. Snow, Gary Snyder, Elvis J. Stahr, Mark Van Doren, Harriet Van Horne, George Wald.

THE LEAGUE OF CONSERVATION VOTERS (LCV)

The League of Conservation Voters has a single purpose: to make sure that environmental issues receive the attention they should before, during, and after elections in the United States. LCV intends to help put into office, and keep there, men and women who are pledged to work in support of the broad purposes espoused by JMI, FOE, and the progressive traditional conservation organizations.

Criteria for support and endorsement:

Basing its decisions upon information supplied by conservation leaders across the nation, LCV seeks to strengthen its political effectiveness in behalf of the environment.

1) LCV considers the incumbent's record on environmental issues. The issues are too interrelated to categorize adequately in a simple list. They include pollution legislation and its enforcement; methods of limiting population growth; restrictions on pesticides and herbicides; land–use planning; setting aside and protecting parks and wilderness; limitation on power generation and consumption; wildlife protection; expediting improved mass transportation; opposition to the inertial addiction to highways, dams, and the SST; and opposition to military operations that poison or otherwise destroy the global ecosystem.

2) The incumbent's service on Congressional committees is weighed. Most attention is given his stand on issues where he has power through his committee assignments. LCV pays particular attention to legislators on committees closest to environmental issues.

3) LCV endorses outstanding candidates whatever their election chances are, but limits active help to a few close races where the contrast between candidates is great.

4) Assurance is sought that the environment will be a major issue in the candidate's campaigning.

5) LCV tries to help an approximately equal number of candidates from both parties—to demonstrate that the environment is a bipartisan concern.

6) If the candidate is not an incumbent, LCV is interested in him if his actions and commitments stand up well under the relevant criteria and those of the challenged incumbent's do not.

Funding: LCV believes that broad public funding of political campaigns is one of the major unfilled needs in the American governmental process, and cooperates with other groups working for improved government in seeking this broadening of the responsibility of paying for campaigns. One of the critical shortages is financial support for organizations doing such work, and LCV welcomes financial support for its own operations as well as for the candidates it is helping. LCV suggests that contributions to candidates be routed through LCV, to be passed on undiminished to the candidates with the reminder that it was concern for the environment that produced the contributions.

Leadership: The directors of FOE, as individuals, also sit as the governors of LCV and appoint a Steering Committee to operate it, taking great care that the committee should reflect the judgment of leaders in major national conservation organizations.

Steering Committee: Marion Edey, chairman and coordinator; George Alderson, Stewart M. Brandborg, Joe Browder, David Brower, Thomas Dustin, Michael McCloskey, Carl Pope, Gary A. Soucie, Lloyd C. Tupling.

Advisory Committee: Paul R. Ehrlich, Robert Richter, Frank Wallick, Mrs. Barlow C. Wotten.

Citizens who have further questions about the LCV program or who wish to support or take part in it, may complete and mail the form that follows.
League of Conservation Voters, c/o Friends of the Earth
917 Fifteenth Street, N.W.
Washington, D.C. 20005

☐ Please send more information about LCV and whom they have endorsed. Enclosed is 50¢ to cover the bare costs.

☐ I enclose $_____ as a contribution to LCV, realizing that funding for its work is important and hard to obtain. ($25 contributions will be appreciated. More is welcome. Contributions of $50 or more entitle contributor to membership in Friends of the Earth)

☐ I can volunteer time to researching for LCV

☐ I am willing to be a volunteer worker in political campaigns.

☐ I volunteer to help raise money for LCV

Name _____

Address _____

City, state, zip code _____

Area code and telephone number _____

(LCV is nonprofit; contributions are not tax-deductible)

John Muir Institute for Environmental Studies

☐ I enclose $_____ for membership.
☐ I enclose $_____ as a contribution but do not wish to join now.

NAME _____

ADDRESS _____

CITY _____ STATE _____ ZIP _____

(Contributions to the John Muir Institute are tax-deductible.)

Friends Of The Earth
John Muir Institute
30 East 42nd Street
New York, N.Y. 10017

Friends of the Earth

☐ I enclose $_____ for membership.
☐ I wish to participate actively from time to time. My special conservation interests are: _____

☐ My own field is: _____
☐ I enclose $_____ as a contribution but do not wish to join now.
☐ I should like to be kept informed of other books in the Survival Series.

NAME _____

ADDRESS _____

CITY _____ STATE _____ ZIP _____

(Contributions to Friends of the Earth are not tax-deductible.)

ADDRESSES FOR JMI, FOE, LCV

Information about any of the three organizations is available at:
ALBUQUERQUE, N.M. (service headquarters), 8016 Zuni Rd., SE 87108
 (JMI Research office), Biology Bldg., Univ. New Mexico 87106
ANCHORAGE, ALASKA, P.O. Box 1977 99501
BONSTETTEN (ZH), SWITZERLAND, JM Bruggen 425, 8906 Bonstetten (ZH)
HONOLULU, HAWAII, 1372 Kapiolani Blvd. 96814
NEW YORK, N.Y. (FOE main office), 30 E. 42d St. 10017
PARIS, FRANCE (European Representative), 52, Avenue des Champs-Elysees, Paris 8
SAN FRANCISCO, CALIF. (JMI main office), 451 Pacific Ave. 94133
SEATTLE, WASH. (Northwestern coordinator), 1624 East McGraw 98102
WASHINGTON, D.C. (LCV main office), 917 15th St. NW 20005

(None of the offices is large; some are corners of desks; all seek help)

JMI MEMBERSHIPS
Regular $50, Supporting $100, Contributing $250, Life $1,000,* Corporate $1,000.
FOE MEMBERSHIPS
Regular $15, Spouse $5, Student $5, Supporting $25, Contributing $50, Life $250,* Patron $1,000.*
*Life and Patron memberships can be billed quarterly.

THE SIERRA CLUB

The Sierra Club was founded in 1892 by John Muir and has its roots in wilderness. Men who knew the wilderness of the Sierra Nevada from their early climbs and exploration there were gathered from professions and university faculties in the San Francisco region to enlist public support in saving from despoliation the two new California national parks, Yosemite and Sequoia. For the club's first sixty years, the preponderance of new members came to the club because of their interest in wilderness exploration. It was Muir's concept that those who knew the wilderness best—especially the Sierra wilderness—would be the most effective in preserving it. From its beginning, the club was concerned with preserving what man could not replace, and was frequently at odds with organizations and policies deriving from the Gifford Pinchot philosophy that everything on the public lands (with particular reference to national forests), was for sale.

The club led in the early battles to enlarge Yosemite National Park and give it better protection; in establishing greater Sequoia National Park and Kings Canyon National Park; blocking relinquishment of key forests in Olympic National Park; was prominent in supporting legislation to set up the Forest Service and the National Park Service; and in setting up the California State Park System.

In 1952, with 7,000 members, the club took on a professional staff and broadened its field of activities. It led in the protection of Dinosaur National Monument from proposed reclamation dams, in initiating the National Outdoor Recreation Resources Review, in saving Grand Canyon from two proposed power dams, in establishing the Redwood National Park, Point Reyes National Seashore, and Fire Island National Seashore. It was the principal supporter of The Wilderness Society in fighting for the National Wilderness Preservation Act, and of the North Cascades Conservation Council in establishing the North Cascades National Park. The club provided major support

ORGANIZATIONS YOU MAY WISH TO SUPPORT

to the Scenic Hudson Preservation Council in legal action to block the proposed Storm King (Cornwall) Project on the Hudson River, achieving in that action the landmark decision that gave standing to organizations representing the broad public interest, as opposed to narrow economic interest, a decision clearing the way for an important series of legal actions in behalf of the environment by the club and by many other organizations; especially the Environmental Defense Fund, the Center for Law and Social Policy, and Ralph Nader's Center for the Study of Responsive Law. Defense of the Grand Canyon lost the club its tax-deductible status, which was clouded in 1966 and revoked two years later.

In 1959 the club embarked upon a major expansion of its publications program and by early 1969 it had published twenty volumes in its award-winning Exhibit Format Series; a score of guidebooks and wilderness volumes; paperbacks derived from them, including the bestselling Paul Ehrlich book, *The Population Bomb;* plus eleven full-page conservation advertisements in major newspapers, chiefly the *New York Times.* The club was conducting wilderness outings all over the world; the membership stood at 77,000.

At this writing (August 1970) the club has accelerated its program of defending the environment in court, and its membership has continued to rise rapidly—now exceeding 100,000. There are Sierra Club offices in San Francisco, Los Angeles, New York, Washington, D.C., Seattle, Tucson, and College, Alaska. The club is closely associated with the tax-deductible Sierra Club Foundation and with Trustees for Conservation, for whom the club's Washington representative registers as a lobbyist.

Individuals interested in joining the club should fill out and send the following form.

The Sierra Club
Mills Tower
San Francisco, California 94104

Name _____

Address _____

City, state, zip code _____

Dues: $5 initiation, plus $12 (reg.), $6 (spouse), or $5 (jr.). Life, $250.

Enclosed is payment for membership in The Sierra Club for:

_____ (name)

_____ (name)

_____ (name)

OTHER CONSERVATION ORGANIZATIONS

The Nature Conservancy (1917)
Stresses the role of private conservation; purchases, manages, and preserves lands of unique ecological value until such time as governmental agencies can assume the responsibility, buy the lands, and free NC funds for repeating the process.

The National Wildlife Federation (1936)
The largest conservation federation in the world, guiding the work of the thousands of affiliated hunting and fishing clubs in the country through their state wildlife federations. Famous for its wildlife stamps and popular publications.

The National Audubon Society (1905)
Draws its strength from the some 100,000 members who care about what happens to birds; and, in caring, number among the staunchest defenders of an environment safe not only for birds, but for people as well. Publishes *the* most beautiful magazine.

The Conservation Foundation (1948)
A non–member organization, itself supported by foundations and individual philanthropists, and instigator of the most vital environmental research and conferences held to date in this country. Helped initiate "The Earth's Wild Places" series.

The Wilderness Society (1935)
Founded by the late Robert Marshall, one of the leaders in developing the wilderness system on the national forests. The Society's 70,000 members are the nation's primary defenders of wilderness, and realize that the defense begins in livable cities.

The International Union for Conservation (1951)
Informally coordinates the work of conservation organizations throughout the world and, through scientific research and reports, attempts to persuade participant and

nonparticipant nations in the development of sound environmental policies.

The Izaak Walton League of America (1922)

Draws its strength from some 55,000 members who care about what happens to fish, and, in caring, number among the staunchest of defenders of an environment safe not only for fish, but for people, who also need clean waters.

The National Parks and Conservation Association (1919)

Founded through the efforts of Stephen T. Mather, first director of the National Park Service, as the National Parks Association. Chiefly concerned with parks, wildlife, and wilderness; 50,000 members; directed by Anthony Wayne Smith.

The World Wildlife Fund

An international community chest for conservation, devoted to trying to save certain animal and plant species from extinction and concerned with the whole ecological web. Raises funds through national appeals in many countries.

THE NATIONAL AUDUBON SOCIETY

A $10 individual membership in the National Audubon Society brings you six issues of *Audubon*. You will in turn be supporting the Society's broad program of conservation education and environmental action. You will be making a commitment to a cause—the Audubon cause, and yours as well.

National Audubon Society
1130 Fifth Avenue
New York, N.Y. 10028

I would like to receive a year's six issues of *Audubon*, and to support, through my annual membership, the programs of the society.

I prefer: ☐ a $10 individual membership
☐ a $12.50 family membership

Name:

Address:

City: State: Zip:

☐ I have enclosed my check or money order.
☐ Please send me a bill.

Multiple-use coupon. What is suggested below may be more than you are accustomed to allocating for conservation, but you may live longer, feel better, and earn more in an environment which your contribution helps speed toward recovery.

David R. Brower, President
Friends of the Earth
451 Pacific Avenue
San Francisco, California

Dear Mr. Brower

What you said in *The Voter's Guide to Environmental Politics* has persuaded me that I should include survival in my budget and support not just one, but several conservation organizations. I have indicated my choices in the list below, and am enclosing one or more checks, as appropriate, which I hope you will distribute for me.

List A: Deductible	Amount
Nature Conservancy	$
National Wildlife Federation	
National Audubon Society	
Conservation Foundation	
The Wilderness Society	
International Union for Conservation	
Izaak Walton League of America	
National Parks and Conservation Assn.	
World Wildlife Fund	
John Muir Institute for Environmental Studies	
Sierra Club Foundation	
Small Towns Institute	
Environmental Defense Fund	
Center for Law and Social Policy	
Center for Responsive Law	

Total: ....$

        For List A
        Make check out for total amount to
        John Muir Institute
           (*deductible*)

List B: Nondeductible	Amount
Friends of the Earth	$____
League of Conservation Voters	____
Sierra Club	____
Trustees for Conservation	____
Zero Population Growth	____
Environmental Action	____
National Coalition for a Responsible Congress	____

Total: ....$_____

        For List B, make check out to
        Friends of the Earth
           (*nondeductible*)

Your name _____

Address _____

City, state, zip code _____

☐ Check here if part of your contribution is a pledge for which you should like to be billed quarterly.

ZERO POPULATION GROWTH is a political action organization attempting to bring about population stability in the United States and the rest of the world. In about 200 regional chapters across the country, ZPG is using political and educational means to achieve its goal of a stable population.

ZPG's basic goal is the repeal of all anti-abortion and anti-contraception laws to make these services readily available to everyone, with societal incentives toward smaller families.

As examples of actions taken in the interest of a diminishing population growth rate, ZPG has:

- —supported bills to liberalize state and federal abortion laws.
- —worked on a campaign for a "lesser Los Angeles."
- —supported Maryland Senator Joseph Tydings' bill to create a Center for Population and Family Planning in the Department of Health, Education, and Welfare, along with funds for manpower training and research.
- —urged Congressman George Brown to run for the U. S. Senate from California and then supported him in his campaign.

You can get in touch with the ZPG chapter nearest you by calling or writing:

Zero Population Growth
330 Second Street
Los Altos, California 94022
415-941-3666

ENVIRONMENTAL ACTION, since Earth Day, has been serving as a Washington-based advocate for environmental groups around the country. Environmental Action has lobbied against the SST and for strong air pollution legislation; joined legal action to ban the use of 2,4,5-T; initiated legal research on other potential suits; testified before Congressional committees on several bills; organized research task forces on several environmental hazards, most notably atomic energy development; published a book of Earth Day speeches; and published a twice-monthly newsletter. In addition, the group has conducted a series of regional conferences, aiding local groups in getting together in more effective regional coalitions.

Environmental Action has excellent contacts on a nationwide basis. This group will be active through its affiliates in the November Congressional elections.

This organization has perhaps the best mailing list of any environmental group in the country.

Environmental Action
2000 P Street, N.W.
Washington, D. C. 20036
Contact: Dennis Hayes
202-293-6960

THE MOVEMENT FOR A NEW CONGRESS is a campus-based organization which has spread from a single campus to approximately 500 schools in a few months. Its objective is to organize student power to change the U. S. Congress.

The Movement for a New Congress is a national coalition of hundreds of college groups which recognize that next fall's Congressional elections provide the best opportunity to reverse war policy and alter national priorities. The Movement's principal resource will be the student and faculty volunteers it recruits and channels across the country. This manpower will be concentrated on key races through national and regional research and coordination efforts.

The national office aids in the establishment and supervision of regional centers and will maintain regular national communications. Area desks will handle mail and phone contact with regional offices and will answer or forward all other inquiries from the states concerned. A small number of highly experienced organizers will work out of the national office, traveling into unorganized states and providing assistance, advice, and training for established centers.

This organization also stores names of volunteer election workers in computer memory banks. If you wish your name and address to be available to candidates seeking workers across the country, send it to the national headquarters.

Movement for a New Congress
136 Palmer Hall
Princeton, New Jersey 08540
Contact: Robert Durkee
609-924-7260

THE NATIONAL COALITION FOR A RESPONSIBLE CONGRESS consists of university and college-based groups attempting to end the war in Southeast Asia through Congressional action. Some of the organizations in this cooperative effort are:

—The Universities National Anti-War Fund (Harvard, MIT)
—The Movement for a New Congress (Princeton)
—The Academic and Professional Lobby for a Responsible Congress (Columbia)
—The National Petition Committee (Rochester)
—Continuing Presence in Washington (Dartmouth)
—The People's Lobby (Smith)

The Coalition is dedicated to electoral politics, and will support all measures aimed at making Congress more responsible. The Coalition does not represent a new national group, but rather a cooperative association of groups already formed and active. The Coalition's main role will be as a coordination and information dissemination unit. Its activities are not limited to members and affiliated groups, but are available to any group whose goals are similar.

National Coalition for a Responsible Congress
3041 Broadway
New York, New York 10027
212-280-4581
or Contact: Press Office
212-280-5052

The Center for Study of Responsive Law

The Center for Study of Responsive Law is an organization established by Ralph Nader to conduct research into violations of the public interest by business and governmental groups.

Contributions to further this work are tax deductible and may be sent to the center at

> 1908 Q Street, N.W.
> Washington, D. C. 20009

The center also engages students and professionals who are willing to donate their time and energies either on a voluntary basis or for extremely modest wages.

Conservation Coupons

The coupons that follow outline a course of action. People who have the time will state their views far better than coupons will, but the coupons can be a first step, and lead to other steps. Coupons are fine, letters are better, and nonalienating letters are best.

In each coupon, we supply the address (unless it is for your own Senators and Member of Congress, whose name your own city hall should know) and a paragraph or two to start you out. We leave it to you to add the "sincerely yours" and your own name and address; we also leave room for you to add your own note, and hope you will.

The mark of the concerned citizen will be the absence of these pages from the back of your book (or your own note, where appropriate, that you wrote your own).

It will help us next time to learn how you made out this time.

To the President

The President
The White House
Washington, D.C. 20500

Dear Mr. President:

I have been reading *The Voter's Guide to Environmental Politics* and hope you have had a chance to read it too. I am impressed with the statement of various environmental problems, and with the solutions put forth in several of the chapters.

The book speaks of the difficulty of getting men in political life to commit themselves in detail in behalf of such proposals as the book makes—or to commit themselves against the proposals.

To respond in detail to the book would require a book in itself, and that might be a good idea. Meanwhile, it seems to me that a clear indication of your thinking on the issues mentioned would be of inestimable value to the world. Could you undertake this?

I share the concern you have expressed in your several statements about the environment; about the population crisis, about a policy for the oceans of the world, and about governmental reorganization that will assure a far more searching review of projects that threaten the environment than was ever before conducted. I am also deeply concerned about some of the steps that have been taken in spite of your statements.

Since whatever happens to this planet happens to all of us, can you suggest steps that I myself could take to help end this crisis?

Coupon 2. To your senators and representatives—or to your candidates to replace them.

Dear   :

I have been reading *The Voter's Guide to Environmental Politics* and hope you have had a chance to read it too. I am impressed with the statement of various environmental problems and with the solutions outlined in the chapters.

The book speaks of the difficulty of getting men in political life to commit themselves in detail to such proposals as the book makes—or to commit themselves against the proposals. But I wonder if you would respond to the book. To respond in detail would require a book in itself, and that may be a good idea. Meanwhile, it seems to me that a summary of your response, or a clear indication of your thinking, would be of inestimable value to your constituency, of which I am one.

Could you undertake this, and could you also suggest steps that I myself could take to help end this crisis?

Coupon 3. To the president of one of the largest corporations in the world. (see Fortune *for August for its list of the biggest ones).*

Dear   :

Having learned from *The Voter's Guide to Environmental Politics* that a man who is obliged to steer the affairs of a major corporation, and who stands a good chance of dying early of excess tension or of ulcers, by virtue of his responsibilities cannot be all bad, I have a question for you: How do you feel about the solutions proposed in the several chapters of *The Voter's Guide?*

I suppose there should be a second question. Since we share a finite planet in which all kinds of growth cannot go on forever without something's bursting, (whereupon we may all leave the planet together) what kinds of growth do you think we must continue, what kind taper off, and what kind reverse?

These questions are extremely difficult; but so is the problem. From your perspective, and with your influence in channeling money, the lifeblood of the economy, you have the opportunity to make a major contribution to not only the economy, but also to survival.

I hope your corporation will consider becoming a corporate member of Friends of the Earth.

Coupon 4.

Mr. Don Clifford
McKinsey & Company
Address
Park Avenue
New York

Dear Mr. Clifford:

As you are a partner of what is perhaps the most prestigious management–consultant firms there is, and since you also are a partner who has shown concern about what is happening to the environment, I am sending you a copy of the letter I just sent to the president of one of the largest corporations.

This corporation may not be a client of yours, but you are probably well aware of their work. Could you let me know what people in consultant work can do to further some new thinking about the problems and solutions set forth in *The Voter's Guide to Environmental Politics*?

Your answer may fill a book. Perhaps Friends of the Earth would be pleased to be joint publisher of it, if that is what happens.

Coupon 5. To the president of a life insurance company.

President
Equitable Insurance Company

Dear   :

I have just read *The Voter's Guide to Environmental Politics* and its presentation of problems and solutions. An idea has occurred to me that ought to interest you. The insurance companies of America, out of sheer self-interest, should be eager to see recovery of the environment take place as rapidly as possible because a sick environment is a bad investment, and people live progressively shorter lives the sicker it gets.

Perhaps you have never looked at it this way, but it seems to me that the conservation organizations of America are in a very real sense doing your work for you and deserve your support—especially those that cannot receive tax-deductible gifts as a charity but which can be recompensed for services given.

Do you see any logic in this suggestion, and could you come to the aid of the environment in such a way?